TREASURES OF THE ANCIENTS

A Field Guide To Lost Treasures And How To Become An Explorer

---

TIMOTHY DRAPER

Treasures of the Ancients
Paperback Edition
Copyright © 2023 Timothy Draper

Wolfpack Publishing
9850 S. Maryland Parkway, Suite A-5 #323
Las Vegas, Nevada 89183

wolfpackpublishing.com

All rights reserved. No part of this book may be reproduced by any means without the prior written consent of the publisher, other than brief quotes for reviews.

Paperback ISBN 978-1-63977-850-8
eBook ISBN 978-1-63977-851-5

Acknowledgments

This book is dedicated to all the people in my life that have supported me. Even when I felt that this way of life was not approved by others, my wife (LeeAnn), my kids, my dad, my mom, and my closest friends supported me. Thank you.

LeeAnn, I know that my work has at times been hard due to the time I have invested. I want you to know that I love you for letting me write this book. This is something that I know I'm ready to do and I wanted to thank you for understanding.

To my mom, I love you and I miss you every day. I will never forget how you supported me and encouraged me to go down the path I chose. I know you are still watching and encouraging me in the afterlife. I know I will see you again. Hopefully when I'm ready and when I have fulfilled my life's work.

I would like to include my dad as well. He was the one that taught me the value of history. Dad, I remember all the questions I had for you as a kid growing up. You always told history just the way I needed to hear it. Your passion became my passion. I love you and I'll continue my research until I'm no longer able to.

Along my path, I lost my great friend and mentor, Steve Shaffer. This book is for you, buddy. I will never forget our friendship and adventures. You helped me understand that it's okay to do what I feel I need to do.

I would like to thank my team members from Treasures in America & Uncharted Expedition. You have stood by me and my passion for years. I couldn't have asked for better friends and partners. Thanks for your support and continued friendship.

TREASURES OF THE ANCIENTS

Introduction

In my life, I've found a purpose and a passion for finding and investigating what I call the *legends of the ancients* and I hope to share this passion with you.

I've always been intrigued by stories of lost riches. There's something about the possibilities that draw me in. Is it wealth? Partly perhaps, but it's also so much more. There's the mystery, the promise of adventure, and most compelling of all—the hunt. These are the things that have motivated me through all the adventures and all the pages of history I've turned in over twenty-six years as a treasure hunter.

Growing up, I watched movies about pirates and about hunting for treasure. I never could have imagined I would choose it as my path—or that it might choose me. As a kid, I would get lost in fantasies of going out to the wilderness to track down lost structures, mines, old documents, and more, but I never considered these were anything more than youthful daydreams.

Hollywood movies like *National Treasure* or *Indiana Jones* are fun and exciting, but what about real life? With an open mind, and the trade secrets and *uncommon* knowledge in this book, you may find your doorway to the treasure hunting adventures you've always dreamed about.

Make no mistake, *Treasures of the Ancients* is about real lost history—however, all things may not be as they seem. The history lessons you think you learned in school are about to get turned on their heads—those were controlled stories, convenient explanations without real evidence or proof.

Are you ready to learn some new information? Then be prepared, because treasure hunting is not easy. In many ways, it is the most challenging of all adventures.

I've spent most of my adult life with my head in archives, in libraries, and speaking with people around the world who think outside the traditional ways. I've learned history has been suppressed, and is even completely wrong at times.

Consider the possibility you may not have been taught the correct history. I have been told in the past that history text books are written so a 5th grader can understand them and so they don't confuse people.

I understand the concept, but if all history is written at a 5th grade level, how can the full story of history be explained and truly understood? I find it strange that the accepted and established norms should be designed to shelter us from the core of historical truths—maybe that's why history can be so confusing and even contradictory at times.

It also could be that the average person doesn't care about history. The glossed over, prepackaged thought control is fine by them, which leaves a lot of room for others to control the storylines and narratives.

I do care, and I've spent my adult life learning all I can about history—in the office, in the field, and in my travels. I tend to lean more toward what I can personally investigate and deem fact or fiction with evidence.

Those things I have seen and learned will be passed on to you in the coming pages. Take what you can and go from there. Don't take my word for it, though. Do your own research. The information here will point you in the right direction, but it will be up to use the information as you see best.

If you're like me, this book will get you thinking and off to a good start on your own path to your own research and studies. Only then will you grow and have the opportunity to make your own discoveries. It's not easy, but nothing worthwhile ever is.

I guarantee once you're done with this book, you will never look at the wilderness or mountain ranges the same way again. You will always see possibilities and adventures in front of you. Maybe you will make a discovery and change history as we know it. I sure hope you do.

I am out to find the truth. I will not stop until I'm no longer be able to go out in the field to investigate. This is my life's work and studies into the world of the unknown and untold.

Come join me…let's unravel history's mysteries together.

Tim Draper
Utah 2022

ONE

Treasure Hunter To Historical Researcher

Have you ever heard the term "treasure hunter?" A treasure hunter is someone who is looking for something of value. Gold and silver are priority number one for most treasure hunters, but there are also other important objects such as artifacts, old maps, and ancient documents out there waiting to be found. Unfortunately, in our modern day society, people tend to stereotype treasure hunters as grave robbers who grab any discovered riches for their own personal gain. Some critics boldly claim treasure hunters destroy historical evidence by removing finds, depriving 'authorized' professionals the ability to properly survey, collate, and study these sites of historically valuable significance.

Many archeologists, anthropologists, and other professionals claim treasure hunters are greedy opportunists and have actively disparage their reputation. However, it should be remembered that amateur explorers and adventurers have long been the types of individuals whose passion for discovery has consistently expanded our understanding of history. Exploration of new worlds has been the topic of conversation for hundreds if not thousands of years. Professionals want to take the credit for finding lost cities and caves of riches, but in reality, it is almost always a treasure hunter, amateur scholar, or weekend adventurer who discovered these sites first. Clearly, there have been numerous incidents of grave robbing and looting around the world, but today this is more prevalent in second and third world countries, and is the work of thieves and criminals, not those of us who seek these treasures for both the thrill of discovery and the altruistic purpose of expanding the world's knowledge and understanding of the past.

Most of the time, criminal grave robbers are people who live in the area and know about the riches. They can and often do take advantage of this knowledge to rob an historical site and then sell the artifacts on the black market, or to a small group of rich collectors. But, while acknowledging the heinous practice of taking historical artifacts illegally exists, let me be clear when I say this is not the actions and intent of either myself or the many great individuals I've spent time with while treasure hunting around the world. My goal, and what I want to share with you, is how we can make a difference by discovering new historical sites and artifacts that will bring new evidence to the table and add to the world's understanding of history.

After twenty-six years of exploring and adventuring, I can tell you that many people enjoy a good adventure and many of them dream of finding something great while they are out in the field. With that appreciation of context, let's consider individuals like you and me who simply enjoy researching and getting out in the great outdoors. We may be referred to, or even label ourselves as treasure hunters, but the truth is if we uncover something of historical importance our instinct and behavior is to report the find to the appropriate entities immediately.

Do not believe everything you hear when it comes to treasure hunting and researching. The community is well over four hundred thousand people strong and it has been increasing by around eight to ten percent every year since 2015. That's the number of people we can record from social media platforms, and that's just in North America. Many of them are good people that really care about history. They dream of making a difference in our world, and just like you and me, they want to be the person who finds something exciting. In Europe, it's even more of a practice and hobby in the normal way of life. In some places in Europe, treasure hunters and explorers are even rewarded for making big discoveries. Their names are included with their discoveries, and an honest finder's fee is often paid out if the finders work appropriately with officials. And unlike what happens occasionally in the United States, explorers are not put in jail.

However, in the United States, more and more people are going back to our country's roots—leaving home to strike it rich, whether it's chasing gold, silver, an old mine prospect, or even buried treasure. History is all around us, but you have to know where to look and how to recognize the clues in order to make a discovery. I receive many emails from others like you and me, who have been researching lost history in their area and are seeking clues to put them on the trail to a treasure trove. The one thing they have in common is almost every email includes the plea, *I need someone who I can trust. If the government found out, they would put me in jail.*

The specter of these threats does little to help the world with discovering new history. To overcome this challenge, we need to work together to change the way people hunt and find the history and the riches that are waiting patiently to be uncovered.

Over a decade ago, I was studying anthropology and history at the local university. My hopes were to study hard and work for a government entity like the Forest Service or Bureau of Land Management. After two years, it was obvious becoming Indian Jones was not like in the movies. I wanted to explore and find new evidence of history never before revealed, but in the bureaucratic position where I was working, my dream of finding a lost city that would change history was circling the drain.

Today, the hope of finding new historical evidence is a difficult challenge. To overcome that challenge you must keep an open mind. Many individuals who graduate from a university today are locked in to robotic like thinking and responses. They have been processed through the same educational conveyor belt system that leads them like sheep to an institutionalized and limited world view.

Finding a new outlet and source of information is key, but how can you learn more about becoming a modern day explorer if you follow the yellow brick road of establishment schools?

The truth is, the school of hard knocks will get you further than any baccalaureate degree in closed thinking. In this book, you will learn about the real world where, if you want to find something that is truly lost, you need to become lost yourself and look where others haven't looked before.

There are no big discoveries left to be found in National or State Parks, which have been hiked and explored by everyone and their mother—up and down the mountains and across the field into the canyons.

Don't start there for anything other than a case study—using those conventional places to see and learn what others have done. Fill your information storehouse by observing what has already been established—what structures look like, how they were built, and the cultures that used them. But then you must branch out from the normal way of thinking, so you can open yourself to see new possibilities and alternate accounts of lost history. Learning from others is a prime way to expand your knowledge if you do not get locked into a closed mindset.

During my early days of researching and dreaming of finding treasures, it quickly became clear there was no hardline handbook or a single path to becoming an explorer and adventurer. It was a journey of self-discovery and a realization we have not been told the whole truth about history. In fact, much of what is taught are misconceptions or even outright lies.

Call it what you want. Our historians got it wrong, our county is trying to protect historic sites, hiding behind the idea that some things are only *need-to-know*. No, they're not. True history is important to all of us. It has been said, *those who do not learn history are doomed to repeat it*. However, if we know the real history, then it might change the way we think as a society.

Why is it important to not take the history we have been taught at face value? Do you think those who control what goes in the history books want us to know everything? No, they don't. The reasons for this will unfold for you through the coming chapters.

There was no half-truth handbook for me, only experiences and other open thinkers to show me the way—the greatest gift I could ever receive.

In the coming chapters, you will learn about lost cities in America, as well as Central and South America. You will soon see that treasures and riches can be found in every hidden byway around the globe. In fact, some of the most famous and richest mines known to man are still hidden—lost in the great outdoors.

Together we will take a fresh look at the first explorers to find America. You will come to understand they had deeper motives than simply proving if the world was round, or learning about other cultures. We'll dive into the era of pirates and sunken ships in the Caribbean, as well as the aftermath of the 1800s and the treasures hidden through the acts of outlaws and bandits.

Treasure and riches have been a part of man's history since the beginning of time. It surrounds us when we're hiking and exploring the outdoors. You pass it as you go through a large mountain range. You will soon see the differences in traditional history and how each country teaches it in a different light. History as we know it is not only misunderstood, sometimes it is completely wrong. In our culture, we don't like to acknowledge the bad things that have happened in the past—unless they we committed by others. But if you don't know the facts, how can you understand and know where to start your search?

So, where do you start your search? Coming up, you will get to read the legend of the map, and discover the tools that will lead you to enlightened understanding. The door has now been unlocked—push it open and prepare to see differently for perhaps the first time.

First, drop the label treasure hunter by the wayside. Claim your identity as an *historical researcher* because that's what you are going to become—a person who uses lost maps, old documents, and newfound historical accounts to find riches lost across time.

You may discover rich mines still filled with gold and silver. You may unlock a hidden location designed to never be found. Maybe you will be the next person called to explain what you have found and discovered. You may change history as we know it. The possibilities are endless. It's up to you to draw the line between your boundaries and limitations. And remember, you have a mandate to help others by sharing your experiences and pointing them in the right direction.

Now, let's get you started in the right direction and on the right path. This book was intended to break down the information from one time period to another. Each chapter will take you deeper and deeper into the untold information. We will start with what type of treasures you can find and explain what to look for. From there, we will come to understand what is classified as a lost document or map and how to find and use them. Then we'll keep going. One step after another.

TWO

Treasures Everywhere

To my surprise, many people reach out to me and ask if there is a treasure in their state they can hunt for. The answer is, yes. I can tell you there's treasure in every state in America.

Many years ago, I asked myself the question, how many treasures are believed to be in America? I spent the next 4 years researching. While expanding my research, I had a lot of help. I was contacted by film production companies and was under contract with different producers for three years. This provided a lot of resources I might not have had otherwise if not for my ties with the producers.

In the filming industry, storyline is key. Our storyline became *what treasures are out there and where are they located?* At one point, we spent a month making a comprehensive list of famous lost treasures, labeling them by state. To my surprise, we found between five and fifteen treasure legends in *each* state. These treasure sites were linked to Native Americans, Spanish explorations, the wars of the past 300 years, and even early explorers in America before Christopher Columbus.

There were also other treasure situations we hadn't considered until after our initial list was compiled—mobster treasures, outlaw loot, and buried treasures left behind by prospectors. The possibilities were endless—more than any of us could investigate in a lifetime.

With so many different types of treasures to be researched, investigated, and discovered in America, you'll instinctively know what you like looking for and what you don't. Depending on the type of treasure you would like to track, you'll have to adapt to different ways of searching.

If you want to track down pirate treasures, you'll have to learn the routes of the ships, where the possible locations of shipwreck are located, learn how to scuba dive, and more. Every treasure category requires a different skill set, equipment, and knowledge. Don't make the mistake of taking on too many different types of treasures at once. You can quickly become overwhelmed with learning different tasks as well as the vast amounts of information you will need to process.

In 2013, I hit a hard time in my research. I had accumulated a vast amount of information, which forced me to take a step back to process the facts, the legends, and more than a few imaginative ramblings with no basis. After a few months, I found myself studying less and going outdoors less and less often. I was being burned out by the work in front of me. There was so much of it. As a result, I quit treasure seeking for over a year. I was lost as to where to start and how to begin. It was simply too much to handle.

I had short-wired the drive I had always possessed. I realized I hadn't had a conversation with anyone about treasures in a long time. I felt disconnected from the life I'd built. While I still had work and responsibilities, it wasn't enough. I had always had a hunger for truth and knowledge, but this gift had been derailed. I needed a reset.

I decided to slow my research down and start with one story. From there, I spent a couple of months on a site. When I had accomplished what my goals were there, I went on to the next story on my list.

I kept this process going for another two years, and before I knew it, I had multiple sites working in sync. I had discovered how to ease into that way of multitasking. Now, I have hundreds of sites where

I've conducted extensive work and have the ability to switch from one to another.

The hard lesson here is don't overwhelm yourself with too much varied research while trying to work too many sites at once. Take your time and grow into it. If you've extended yourself too much, you can lose sight of what you're trying to accomplish. You might want to start with simple web searches related to treasure hunting in your state. Use keywords or phrases, such as *best-lost treasures in Utah*.

However, understand this is not a get rich quick scheme. If you're looking for something to make you rich next month, treasure hunting most likely isn't going to be what makes your dreams come true. The reality of treasure hunting is it's time-consuming and expensive. I spent my first 8 years slowly buying the equipment I needed while researching old documents related to my area of interest.

Later in this book, you will find a listing of lost treasures for every state in America. Many of these stories and legends are known and talked about on the web. Look for your state and surrounding states as a starting point. Choose your treasure hunting according to your interest and your preferred location.

The listings will get you started on your journey. Start small and go from there. If you're a beginner, get a backpack, water bottle, good hiking shoes, a GPS system, and a starting point on the map. Learn about the story you have chosen and keep your eyes out for anything unnatural. Think of treasure hunting as a common-sense type of activity.

Think about how you would bury something valuable in the wilderness, and go from there. Would you create a map? Would you leave clues? Would you place it in a commonly known area? Would you intend to come back for it?

When it comes to looking for clues and treasures, begin by keeping it simple. If you suspect someone of concealing something of value in a specific canyon, but can clearly see a horse would likely not make the journey, then the treasure most likely would not be placed there. It's true you would want to hide it in a good hiding place, but remember, back in the day, things were different. Many people who hid something valuable 100 years ago, didn't have cars, roads, and trails to lead them in the right direction.

Just because you can drive to an area today, get out of your car, and hike another fifteen miles, doesn't mean the treasure will be in the hard-to-reach place you are imagining. What took you thirty minutes to drive today may have taken the person with valuables two days on a horse and two days in the wilderness to locate a safe place to bury or hide the treasure. Don't start off with too many complicated thoughts. Start easy and get to know the area. Drive your four-wheel drive through the area the first couple of times, stopping often to get out and pay attention to the landscape, outcroppings, and canyons.

Use a 7.5-minute topographic map to get familiar with the area. Look for caves, and mines, and use *Google Earth* for finding possible structures or anything that appears to be man-made. Take your time. Always treat the situation like you are going to find the treasure. It could be a million-dollar victory or it could be a million-dollar mistake. Always trust your instincts and research. Do not second guess yourself. If you feel you put in enough hours and research, assume you're on the right track. Use all of your senses when you are in the field and your brain will make calculations you might not have consciously picked up. If you feel clues or the landscape are taking you somewhere, follow the lead!

THREE

How To Look For Lost Records & Documents

Finding clues to point you in the right direction is one of the most difficult parts of treasure hunting. To give you a head start, here are some suggestions to save you time and effort.

Old maps and documents are key to real clues. Not all sites and stories will land you on either of those, but it's crucial to first look for these clues. If you have an old map displaying the area and location of where you want to search, it's much easier than starting from scratch. Even if you have an old map, you may never find what you are seeking from it alone. However, old treasure maps will help you see the landscape and natural landmarks as they were in the past, which will provide other clues to get you closer to the area of riches.

Those who hid treasures did not usually do it in their backyard. In the 1800s and 1900s, once towns and homesteads started in the old west, land was scarce in highly populated areas. So, it's pragmatic to assume that if an outlaw wanted to bury a cache, they would look to the vast areas outside the immediate area, especially if he or she had a lot of time to plan the hiding place.

The problem was, if they hid it too well, they may not be able to relocate their valuables again, so cryptic maps became the key to knowing where the goods were stashed. This is clearly a boon to any modern treasure hunter, especially if you know what to look for when it comes to common clues.

I've spent most of my life in the woods and wilderness, but even when I think I know an area very well, mother nature will often prove me wrong. There are some areas where I've spent over twenty years on the same mountain range. Year after year exploring the hillsides, canyons, creeks, and valleys. To my surprise, I can still get turned around and lost in a little canyon I've not explored well. I use natural landscapes to keep my location such as a mountain peak, or a simple creek running in one direction. These are great helpers—until they are not.

Once, I was in the Uinta Mountains of Utah, an area I felt I knew as well as my own backyard. The problem is, landscapes can change very quickly. Weather, rain, snow, and other natural forces can change the landscapes within hours. One day, I was out hiking along an old horse trail. The trail was supposed to lead me to an old Spanish mine. I followed it during good weather and sunshine almost the whole day. Then bad weather moved in very quickly and a hard rain poured down for over an hour. Because of the rain, the colors in the mountains changed. It made the trail muddy and had even washed areas of it away. Outcroppings and the wild grass also change appearances. Before I knew it, I felt like I was walking through an area I'd never been in before.

The rain had changed my perspective of the woods. In just a short time, I completely lost the trail and any clues it might provide. I knew my bearings due to topo maps and my GPS system, but all I could do was head back to camp for the rest of the day. My search was over and I had to rethink my next steps.

The next day, I picked back up from where I'd left off the day before. I found the trail and some tree symbols due to the nice weather. There was no rain that day and I was able to successfully hunt for clues, but I had learned that everything can change in an instant, even for an experienced outdoorsman. Now, if this happened to me after twenty years of exploring this area, what might have happened to someone trying to hide a treasure in the same situation without the same tools at their disposal? I guarantee they, too, would experience the same disorientation.

Many people wonder how it is so many treasures are still lost today. Keeping the above example in mind, understand there could literally be hundreds of different situations that might keep someone who hid a treasure from finding it again.

For another example, imagine you're a Spanish prospector up from Mexico. Picture yourself in the woods, mining and digging tunnels searching for gold and silver. You've lived in the area all summer and you know the good hunting places for food. You know where to get drinking water and where your camp is. Life is good as a miner, but things start to change. Perhaps local native Indians have been coming into your area, and you know a fight is coming. They don't want you on their lands, or are fearful of having their people enslaved.

All summer, you've been storing your gold and silver in a hiding place. Sometimes it was in the mine itself, or sometimes in a nearby cave. It might even have been protected by other Spaniards in the camp. If you knew a local native tribe was coming for you and it was only a matter of time before you would find yourself in a battle, you would most certainly be worried about the safety of your hard won ore.

What would you do with your gold and silver?

You'd most likely want to get it back to Mexico for yourself and your king. That was the way it worked back then. You may have already sent a letter with a rider back to Mexico letting others know you might soon be under attack. But how do you keep your gold and silver? You can either hide it in the area and flee, or you can try to get it out of the area.

Traveling down the known trails back then was a dangerous

time. Gold and silver are heavy and horses and mules can only carry up to a couple of hundred pounds of ore each. If you had 400 silver bars and 120 gold bars, along with a hundred pounds of valuable ore, that would take roughly around 62 horses and/or mules to carry your valuables to Mexico. To pull this off, you would need close to forty men to manage the mule train and successfully move your payload from Northern Arizona to Mexico City. Traveling heavily like this would slow down the group and only allow maybe ten miles of traveling per day. If the group traveled from Prescott, Arizona, to Mexico City, it would be over 1500 miles to reach your destination. At the rate of ten miles per day, it would take close to five months to arrive in Mexico City—and that's without any problems along the way.

The roads were very dangerous back then. If you're packing a heavy payload of valuables along the main trails, word would get out very fast, and the temptation to relieve you of your gold and silver would be overwhelming for some. Because of this, traveling would be even slower. Your compatriots would be on high alert for the full five months, and most likely you would see many battles that could add weeks to your journey, if not wipe your party out.

History shows that for over 150 years, the Spanish had to consider these circumstances during times of travel. They had their guns and armor, but the native Indians were masters at ambushing and using battle techniques in their favor. Eventually, if became clear that less than 10% of the Spaniards' gold and silver ever hit the city roads of Mexico City.

This is where lost treasures come from. This is information you can understand and use in your favor. You have to ask yourself, did the Spanish get their treasure out of the woods, or did they stand their ground and protect their valuables in the area where the gold and silver sources came from.

The answer is…most of the gold and silver ended up staying in the area of the mines. So, in thinking about the information in this chapter, where do you logically think they put their valuables?

The Spanish had rules and regulations for hiding treasures. Some believe they would always bury their treasures six feet deep in the ground. This may be true to a point, but there's more to it. Not all of the Spaniards' valuables ended up buried in the ground. As mentioned earlier, some mines had a vault room—a virtual safe where they locked the gold and silver behind sturdy, thick wooden doors with lock and key. Some ended up in a secret cave location. The possibilities are as diverse as you can imagine.

So, how do you find their treasures?

The clues and landmarks, etc. mentioned early in the chapter now come into play. The Spanish did have many treasure symbols and rock monuments they used for re-locating treasures. These clues were well known to other Spaniards in case the original team never made it out of the wilderness. That way, any Spaniard team could come back to find the treasure of their lost companions. This scenario happened more often than not. The Spanish were driven by greed, and the Native Americans hated the Spanish for that fact and many other reasons.

Later in the book, Spanish symbols, rock monuments, and Spanish treasure clues will be revisited, but for now, simply begin by trying to think like a treasure hunter. How could you use maps, old documents, and history itself to locate a treasure hidden by the Spaniards?

Think about things like letters to Mexico and the riders who carried them...This could be your first clue. The Spanish kept writers in every group who understood the ways to explain the news of battles, discoveries, failures, and successes. These records can still be found today. A treasure hunter who has time and money could travel to Mexico right now and start their own research—as has been done many times before.

But there are many unknown maps and records the Spanish still kept in Mexico City today and even in Spain itself. The kings of Spain always required they be advised of all news in the new world. These records and maps were saved and stored for use at later times. Many treasure hunters have spent their lifetime looking for these documents so they can get an inside look into the history of Spanish treasures. If it's possible, consider finding an experienced mentor who has spent a lifetime of searching. These old maps and documents are held by many countries whose governments are still protecting them for historical purposes. Many successful treasure hunters have bought and paid for these documents to have in their homes to study and learn from.

These old maps and documents are more valuable than you know, so it won't be easy to recover them. Sometimes it's who you know and how much money you have when it comes to acquiring these documents, but luck is still required. If treasure hunting was easy, everybody would be doing it. There'd be no value to treasure hunting because everything would already have been found. But that is not the case as we know many treasures are still lost today.

There are thousands of different scenarios about treasures that belonged to the Spanish, the French, the British, outlaws like Jesse James, and so much more. If you are devoted and work hard learning the old techniques and legends, and by then using old maps and documents, you could be on your way to finding lost history and riches.

Treasure clues have been used for thousands of years by many different people and cultures. Outlaws used the same technique in the 1800s. The British also used treasure clues. Even Hitler did the same. You have to accept the fact that no one would hide valuables without documenting a way to come back to claim them. No one!

Never give up your research and never assume the valuables and treasures you are seeking have been found until your research tells you it is no longer discoverable.

Most of the time it takes field searching to conduct this type of discovery. If you want to be successful, learn how to manage your time in the library and archives and balance your field research. This is how you will grow and become a successful treasure hunter.

If you take on the task of looking for information to obtain old maps and documents, plan on spending a lot of time and some money to do so. Reading books from old-time treasure hunters is a great way to learn more information, and the world wide web can help you, too. Spend your time wisely and learn to decipher the difference between simply a good story and a story that has definitive clues to help you learn new information. Don't sell yourself short. Take your time, put in the needed work, and be confident in your best efforts.

FOUR

History And The Differences

Good old history. History is so important because it's a way to learn what others have done before us. It can teach us about mistakes and it can teach us about success. Getting to know your history is something we all should take to heart.

Who controls history?

It's the people who get to make the choices of documenting what happened and what didn't. As a result, the history you know and were taught is flawed. It's from an environment controlled by a select few who can change the narrative to fit their own purposes.

For example, in school we were told Christopher Columbus was a man who wanted to prove the earth was round, not flat. At best, that scenario is a children's story and nothing else. Christopher Columbus was able to get one of the most powerful countries in the world to help him discover the new world. Spain at the time was on a mission that lasted hundreds of years in an effort to conquer the world. They claimed they did it for glory and God, but that was only a way to use religion to their benefit.

We're talking about a country that completely wiped ancient cultures off the face of this earth. There are so few Mayans left in the world today because of the Spanish. The same for the Aztecs. Again erased from history. Their language, methods, and people are now almost extinct.

We're still using anthropology and archeology to understand their cultures after 500 years due to the Spanish. Go to Mexico and ask locals how they feel about American history. They will tell you that our history is wrong and who are we to say what is what? Mexico should be able to tell its own story, not America.

America is a great country, but we as the people know very little about the real history of the world. People like me are told we're wrong and heading on a bad path of research. If my research tells me the accepted history is wrong, then I'm going to go where history I'm uncovering tells me to go—the real history.

Take a look at Native Americans in North America. We wonder why they don't want to be a part of our culture. Who's the terrorist? Native Indians that owned these lands or the Europeans who took them from the Indians? Would you allow someone to come to your home and take it without a fight? Of course you wouldn't.

Spain only cared about gold, silver, spices, and other valuables. They had a financial situation that needed to be filled with power. This is why you are not told this in school. Does history make a country like Spain prosper in today's world when their success was accomplished by the spilled blood of cultures around the world? It would not be tolerated in today's world. Spain today is one of the worst countries when it comes to crime. Try to go to Spain and walk down the streets with your American jewelry and credit cards. Many Americans are attacked for having those things in Spain.

So why is history suppressed?

It's because those in power want to stay in power. Big organizations want people to know only what they want you to know. Keep it simple… Control the environment… Keep the power…

If I took my local state's history at face value, I would be looking for Spanish treasures in Arizona or New Mexico. My experiences tell me it's the same way no matter what state you live in. This makes it hard for an explorer or treasure hunter because if you go off the textbooks, you'll never go to an area with real potential for finding treasures. You may never know the real story. Do your own research. Take textbook stories with a grain of salt, and investigate firsthand.

Meeting like-minded people is a great starting point. You may be surprised by other people's information. This is what gave me my big start. In fact, at first, I didn't think other people's information was correct. Why would I? It's not what I learned in school.

The brain is a powerful thing. If you have been told your whole life that something is what it is, then you'll grow into that way of thinking. I want to open your mind. Only then can you start your journey into the unknown. If you want to find something that's truly lost, you need to become lost yourself.

The reason I am pressing this topic so hard is because I feel you will be more successful in finding lost treasures if you know what to look for. If you stick to your local history, there's a very good chance you may miss out on other stories and lost history. But, as you follow the trail and come across and start to really dig metaphorically in areas and stories that are not as well-known, you could make a great discovery.

Sticking to the common information will only get you a common discovery. I enjoy a real hunt. I don't go geocaching. I don't attend scavenger hunts because I feel they don't challenge my abilities. I like to start my hunt from the beginning and treat my research as an investigator.

Did you know Hitler tried to crash the American dollar and economy in World War II? That's right, and he didn't do it from Europe. He had people in America help to smuggle gold into the country and cache it in secret places. His plan was to bring in millions of dollars' worth of gold and sell it all at the same time to make the value of gold plummet. This would have crashed the American economy and devalued our all the gold reserves stored at Fort Knox. To make a long story short, America would then not have had the money to fund the war. Hitler was unsuccessful. Luckily our secret services caught on and put an end to his plan by arresting and imprisoning the American collaborators.

Have you ever heard this story before?

There's proof and evidence this actually happened. First, you have to know the story then you can investigate it. But you also need to understand what to look for in your studies. Here are two clues. Look into the *Lue Map*. This map is a Freemason map created not by the Freemasons themselves, but by local Hitler loyalists who happened to be Freemasons.

Hitler knew the Freemasons used symbols only another Freemason would understand. This makes the map a challenge to decipher. I've spent time with Freemasons and none of them will tell me if this is possible or not. Their society is very closed-mouthed and if you're not a part of their club, you will have difficulty getting the answers you seek. The key to doing so, however, is research, research, and then doing more research...

The second clue is a secret mansion Hitler was building for himself in the north east of America. I know it sounds implausible, but what if it's true? I've spent some time reaching out to people I worked with at the Discovery Channel in 2015, while putting together a television show. Working with a large network allowed me to have more resources than I was able to previously access. Many people are willing to give information away when they feel their hard work will be shown on tv. It was during this time I came to believe in Hitler's American mansion.

Somewhere in North America, a foundation to a huge mansion is all you can see today. The construction started, but ended when the war ended. If you were able to find more, you could be on your way to changing history and making a huge discovery.

You will not find this information in a history book. This type of research has been conducted by scholars. If I didn't mention it in this book, it could be safe to say you may have never heard about this story. Is it true? That is up to you to find out. I have released the information and now you can do your own research and come to your own conclusions.

Here's another point, and I've only experienced this by traveling to different countries, talking to people of their culture and history. Let's take Mexico for example. I've learned American history is much different from the history taught in Mexico. A good friend of mine grew up in Mexico City until he was 17 years old. He came to the United States for the opportunity to grow financially and better his family's life. When he acquired his United States citizenship, he had to learn English. He later became a contractor in construction. He told me he had to teach himself how to read and write English so he could pass his contractor's test. He is truly a devoted hard worker. After over 30 years now, he still remembers the history lessons he learned in schools in Mexico.

He told me there was a big difference between the history he learned in Mexico and what we believe here. He said Mexico teaches that the history of the Aztecs, Mayans, and other ancient cultures was based on stories passed down from one generation to the next—but here in the United States those ancient histories are told strictly from an American perspective, one that varies greatly from what was truly passed down firsthand.

I've asked myself, how can American histories claim to know the record of the ancient Hispanic cultures better than the people who grew up in the area? Could it be that there are two different stories being told?

I do know this, if I was investigating a new story, I would go to the source. If there was a lost treasure in a certain area, I would go talk to people who grew up there with a couple of generations of their families in the area. I would reach out to those locals and get the stories that have been passed down for generations. A lot of information can get twisted; somebody says I heard a story from a guy who knows a guy versus a story sacredly passed down from one generation to another within a family unit.

When I research a new story, I always hope and plan to find people whose families had a piece of that history, in the area where they grew up. This is prime. I've had much better luck with cracking and solving a treasure story with locals as opposed to working with others who didn't live in the area, who only *think* they have the correct story. This is a good point for you to remember. When you research, try to find people with stories who were actually involved —either personally or through a direct family member. Family history is usually conducted differently than normal history. It's personal to the family members and they tend to take more pride in their history versus an outsider.

It seems to me Mexico would know more about their country's history than the United States. In fact, if you can read books written by Mexican historians, be sure to read that before a book that was written by someone who doesn't live in Mexico. Sometimes using common sense will get you further in historical research. Bottom line —if possible, get your information from the horse's mouth, so to speak.

As soon as I learned the difference between history text books and history books written by authors who have done their own research, my research process changed. I was no longer bound by guidelines and information everyone can obtain. My research flourished, and before I knew it, I had leads to many lost sites with possible riches that weren't in normal history books.

I will say, be aware of authors and treasure hunters who tell fish stories. It's not necessarily done on purpose, but some treasure hunters get hooked on a story and can't let it go. Many treasure hunters make the mistake of grabbing onto a single story and then spend a lifetime searching for fortune and glory. I learned just because a person seems credible, it doesn't mean they are.

If you truly want to find lost treasures and history, you need to research and explore in the wilderness before you spend a lifetime committing to any single legend or folk story. When I started out, I stuck to history that was already known by many others. I spent several years starting where someone else ended. That was a mistake for me. I learned I needed to find lost history of which others weren't aware. I figured the treasure stories that were already known, meant many other hunters has already explored the area.

Think of it like a fisherman. Some fishermen say, "It's my fishing hole and I won't tell you where it is." Treasure hunters are the same way. I know I am. I will not give out secret information to a stranger, especially if there's a possible discovery in the works.

Another thing to look out for is false information and hoaxes. I don't know why, but here in Utah and some surrounding states, someone, or maybe a group of people, have carved fake symbols on rocks and trees. Someone has built rock monuments and even carved fake hieroglyphs. These types of possible clues are hard for most of the general population to date. This gives a perfect situation for false information leading nowhere.

I can't even begin to tell you why someone would do this. I have a few ideas, but I can't prove it. Let's just say some people want their information to be correct so much, they have hoaxed their discoveries. Religion and beliefs can be very strong in some people. Even enough to fake clues and historical sites to look and feel as if they are historically real. Some have written books about these fake sites, and some have created social media groups and websites about their false discoveries. It's hard to figure out why, but beware—it's out there.

I have visited many of these places others have referred to as a real treasure site only to determine the clues are way too modern. Later in this book, I'll teach you how to do a field test using lichen, as well as a rough test with tree carvings to get an approximate date when the tree carvings were made.

The point I am trying to make is *be an investigator*. Become a detective and try to prove or disprove these types of things. Not everything you read and hear is truth! It is up to you to determine what you are willing to spend your time on.

FIVE

Treasure Clues Are Disappearing

The key to being a successful treasure seeker is to find the clues left by the original person involved in hiding the valuables. This means understanding what to look for and what each clue means. That is getting harder to do as many clues lost history and treasures are fading as people with pertinent information pass away. But it's not just time.

People are also uncaringly destroying clues and lost history every day. I've visited uncountable sites and found someone before me had destroyed a rock monument, petroglyph panel, old structures, and more. Some people don't know any better; kids out in the wilderness being kids, and some who should know better just don't care.

Kids in the wilderness are a particular problem. Sometimes it's just kids being kids. Sometimes it goes further with older kids who go out to the wilderness to drink alcohol and do crazy things—not even knowing they just destroyed a Native American panel that had been there for over 1,200 years. I have found bullet holes in rocks where hieroglyphs are embedded, and spray painted graffiti at sites with early Spanish writings on the walls. To some kids, it's fun to be rambunctious and destroy objects with their friends, making this type of destruction virtually impossible to stop. However, we can do our part by teaching our own kids to respect history. We need to tell them about and show them historical sites so they can understand.

Once evidence of history is gone, it's lost forever. But those treasure clues that remain are all meant to be understood by a certain group and/or person who want to retrieve the treasure. Basically, they hid their treasure so well even they couldn't find it again without their own clues pointing the way.

Rock monuments—piles of rocks creating a structure—are often designed to give meaning or direction. They can come in many different shapes and sizes. They can have many different meanings. The rule of thumb is, the bigger the rock monument, the further away you are from the treasure. As you get closer to the treasure, the rock monuments almost always get smaller. This is one way to know if you're getting close.

If a rock monument is 8-feet-tall, you could be anywhere from three to ten miles away. If a rock monument is small, say 2-4 feet, then you can assume you're 3 miles away or less. The big monuments are usually trail markers. Big enough for you to see from a long distance while on foot or on horseback. They usually rest on a hilltop or at the beginning of a canyon to help show the right direction. As you continue to travel keep a sharp eye out for smaller rock piles.

These types of treasure clues are fast disappearing, now more than ever. As cities and roads continue to be developed, these types of treasure clues are discarded and destroyed in the process.

What's infuriating, however, is when other, mostly newbie, treasure hunters purposely destroy these types of clues because they believe the treasure is buried underneath the rock structure. This is almost always a false assumption. There is always a small possibility of treasure being buried underneath, but most of the time, rock monuments are clues to get you closer to the treasure. Much more often, it is rock carvings and tree symbols than can tell you if there's a treasure under something.

As you can see from the picture above, the rock piles are smaller with one pointing to another, which points to the next. This site had over 100 rock monuments and 90% of them pointed to another one. This is a directional rock marker or rock monument. Only 10% of the 100+ rock monuments pointed to a nearby mountain peak. The way we knew that was by painstakingly following them, one by one, and learning over time what the meanings were of each one. These types of treasure clues have been used for over a thousand years all around the world. Once you learn what they indicate when you find them in the field, you'll be closer to recovering treasure.

Tree symbols are another type of clue that is disappearing over time. Nature and man are helping them disappear quicker than ever. But, again, it is other treasure seekers who know what the symbols mean and will cut down the tree to stop others finding it or even simply to save the symbol in a collection. Sometimes a treasure hunter will find a tree with symbols and cut it down to sell to people willing pay for its historical value. Unfortunately, this has become a very popular practice in the past few years.

The previous picture isn't your ordinary natural tree marker. It takes a keen eye to tell the difference. If you look closely, you can see knife marks on the trunk of the tree. You can also see bark is growing over the marking. This is one of the oldest tree markings I've seen in my lifetime. All we know is its most likely Spanish and is most likely pointing to a treasure somewhere ahead. This is a good example of what to look for while you're in the field.

Most pine trees live between a hundred up to a thousand years. Our forbearers knew this and that's why it's typical to find treasure symbols on pine trees. Often whatever trees in the area of the hidden treasure that looked healthy and strong were chosen to carve symbols, knowing the tree would last long enough for someone to return and recover the treasure.

In some cases, I've seen symbols on odd trees within the landscape—trees that stand out from the others. These were easy to mark on a map. Natural landmarks like a standalone tree or a very tall tree are choosing as being more noticeable.

But once time, or fires such as lightning strikes, kill trees, they fall over and weather away. Beyond these natural occurrences, trees can be cut down for lumber, to clear the ground, or for other reasons of modern "progress."

Consider a group of Spanish miners who found a mineral deposit, dug a mine tunnel, but the winter came in and they had to leave. The Spanish would carve symbols in the healthy nearby trees to give clues to the whereabouts of the mine location. You may find more than 10 symbols in a group of trees. They could also be spread out over a couple miles. These symbols were meant for future compatriots to come back and find the mine entrance or a buried cache that had to be abandoned.

In case they themselves didn't make it back, the Spaniards who originally carved the tree symbols would have had a cartographer create a map to point to the tree clues, but not necessarily the mine itself.

Luckily some treasure hunters can understand some of these clues because the meaning and technique have been passed down through generations. Without the knowledge of the meanings, you won't figure out much other than you might be within a couple miles of a mine, treasure, or something else valuable.

Tree symbols, like rock monuments, are very important to treasure seekers and explorers—usually pointing toward something bigger. I know of over 200 symbols that are used on trees and rocks. Some are used to point you in a direction. Some will tell you where the treasure is buried, or how deep in the ground it is, and some are used to confuse you and send you in the wrong direction. These symbols can be very tricky and it takes time and patience to figure out what their meanings are.

The biggest point of this chapter is to explain how many clues are soon going to be gone. For example, if Jesse James buried his loot and marked a nearby tree with a carving in 1870, the tree, no matter how strong it was, is now over 150 years old. Maybe the tree was burnt by forest fires. Maybe it died from old age or was clear cut. With its disappearance, the clue to the loot disappeared with it.

Most of my research in North America is on old Spanish explorations. Some of these Spanish stories date back to the 1600s in North America. That would make some treasure sites over 400 years old; any tree carvings would now most certainly be gone never to be found again.

I also have many years of experience hunting for outlaw treasures. These individuals weren't as organized as the Spanish. Most of the outlaw treasures were buried or hidden in a hurry due to the law or other outlaws pursuing them. So, their treasure clues, symbols, or rock monuments weren't built with a lot of integrity. In my last 25 years of research, I've found treasure clues and a few years later, I return to that site to further my hunt, only to find the clues gone due to man or nature.

Here's another terrible thing that can happen to treasure clues. Sometimes nature can be destroyed because of growth. About 10 years ago I was told a story that was purportedly known by only a few old timers in the Southern Utah area. The location of the Spanish massacre site in the story was given to me. I didn't know if the tale was real or not, so I took a very small team to investigate. Within a day, we discovered the old trail and followed it up the high mountains for over twenty miles. We came across a natural landmark that the old timers had mentioned—a mountain peak made of solid granite. It was obvious to us we had found the right location as described.

We left the four-wheeler by the hilltop and started to explore. The minerals looked good to me, so we used our metal detectors to look for gold deposits. Within about 30 minutes, we found very small gold deposits in the ground, just a few inches deep. Now, we believed we were in the right area, but I had to make sure.

We hopped back on the four-wheelers and traveled further down the dirt trail for three miles. We started to find small rock monuments. Remember, small rock monuments mean something valuable is close. Even though we didn't uncover the site of where local Native Indians massacred the Spanish prospectors, nor were we able to find the gold mine, we still believe to this day that we were within a mile radius of the location.

I'm including these pictures below so you can see how treasure clues are important and how time is destroying these clues.

Treasures of the Ancients | 33

Figure 1- Red rock monument overgrown

Figure 2- Illustration of the rock monument. The pointer rock at the top shows the direction of travel.

Figure 1 is the red rock monument we found. It has a pointer rock at the top of the monument to point in the direction of travel(figure 2). In figure 1, you can see how the vegetation has been growing around the rock monument. Most likely the Spanish didn't build it in the vegetation. Most likely, the rock monument was built in an area clear of vegetation, but time has allowed mother nature to reclaim the space.

The vegetation is very thick around the rock and the brush is actually starting to push and destroy the monument to the point it will most likely disappear within a few more years.

This is area is where the Spanish explored Utah. This could very well show the Spanish massacre story to be true, and that the area needs more investigation. There is a real possibility old mines, burial sites of the Spanish, or a bigger treasure are somewhere in this area.

This is an important site, but time and nature will eventually wipe the clues away, making it impossible to find the secrets locked away in the area. Because I'm currently researching and hunting for a discovery at over one hundred sites, I will tell you where this site is.

I would rather share the location so others may have the chance to unlock its mystery than allow time to destroy the clues. If you go to Utah and travel to the town of Veyo, you will be about 30 miles away. From Veyo, travel to the northwest to what is called Cove Mountain. Look for the peak that is barren of trees and made of granite. From there take the four-wheeler trail to the northwest about 1 mile and look to your right as you start to approach the down-hill dirt road. The site is located along the *Bull Valley OHV Trail 31003* around coordinates 37°24'55.92"N, 113°49'53.02"W.

I hope this shows you I mean business when it comes to treasure clues disappearing over time. I gave up one of my personal sites because I feel my time at this site has come and gone. I want someone to find the clues and unlock this mystery.

The old timer told me that back in the 1700s, the Spanish found rich gold and silver deposits in the area. They started to mine for several years. The gold and silver was piling up and the Spanish took nearby Indians as slaves to work the mine. After time, Indian warriors set out to get rid of the Spanish. Their mission turned into a battle and the small group of 7 Spaniards were killed and buried in a shallow grave. The mine, gold, and silver were left due to the Indians not wanting anything to do with it. The Indians called gold *The White Man's Sickness*. They had no reason to take it as they had no use for it.

In our lifetime and definitely in our children's lifetime, many potential treasure sites will be unrecognizable and the clues to finding riches gone forever. The time for new discoveries is now and treasure hunters are needed more than ever. It's not just the variables that will disappear. It's also the history and stories that will disappear.

History shows many discoveries have been made by people like you and me. In fact, many archaeological sites in modern times have been discovered by locals who knew the legends and stories. It's usually someone like us who points the way for historians and anthropologists. We need to understand the significance of these sites before it's too late.

SIX

Lost Cities In America

Lost cities in America sounds like an action movie, such as *National Treasure*. But lost cities are real—cities not found on any map of America. These sites are not somewhere you pay a fee to see. These are sites lost to time, hidden from the general public.

But how did these cities get lost, or even more specifically, who or what caused them to vanish?

Back in the early 1900s before the Grand Canyon became a National Park, two men rode the Colorado River from Lake Powell to Lake Mead. The whole river was reconnoitered by G.E. Kincaid, a contracted archaeologist hired by the Smithsonian to explore and document the area we now know as the Grand Canyon.

Kinkaid was well-known for exploration. After spending some time in the Marble Canyon of the Grand Canyon, Kinkaid noticed a ledge about two thousand feet up the cliff walls. He felt the ledge could have been manmade. He and his assistant decided to pull the boat out of the Colorado River and hike up to the ledge to investigate.

Once they climbed to the ledge, they found themselves about fifteen hundred feet from the top of the ridge.

That is a clue to this story. Cliff walls are usually about three thousand feet tall from the river to the rim of the Grand Canyon. Kincaid claimed to have been in the Northern end of the Marble Canyon.

After further exploration, Kinkaid found a cave opening and decided to explore the interior. Upon inspection of the cave's entrance, he noticed the ledge and some of the features of the cave were indeed manmade. A little further into the cave opening, he found something that would change the way we think about lost cities in America. He found an underground city that  belonged to ancient culture who abandoned it many years before Kincaid would uncover it.

This is what the *Arizona Gazette* news article said in 1909:

> *The latest news of the progress of the explorations of what is now regarded by scientists as not only the oldest archeological discovery in the United States but one of the most valuable in the world, which was mentioned some time ago in the* Gazette, *was brought to the city yesterday by G.E. Kinkaid, the explorer who found the great underground citadel of the Grand Canyon during a trip from Green River, Wyoming, down the Colorado, in a wooden boat, to Yuma, several months ago.*
>
> *According to the story related to the* Gazette *by Mr. Kinkaid, the archeologists of the Smithsonian Institute, which is financing the expeditions, have made discoveries that almost conclusively prove that the race which inhabited this mysterious cavern, hewn in solid rock by human hands, was of oriental origin, possibly from Egypt, tracing back to Ramses. If their theories are borne out by the translation of the tablets engraved with hieroglyphics, the mystery of the prehistoric peoples of North America, their ancient arts, who they were, and whence they came, will be solved. Egypt and the Nile, and Arizona and the Colorado will be linked by a historical chain running back to ages which staggers the wildest fancy of the fictionist.*
>
> *Under the direction of Prof. S. A. Jordan, the Smithsonian Institute is now pursuing the most thorough explorations, which will be continued until the last link in the chain is forged. Nearly a mile underground, about*

1480 feet below the surface, the long main passage has been delved into, to find another mammoth chamber from which radiates scores of passageways, like the spokes of a wheel.

Several hundred rooms have been discovered, reached by passageways running from the main passage, one of them having been explored for 854 feet and another 634 feet. The recent finds include articles that have never been known as native to this country, and doubtless, they had their origin in the orient. War weapons, copper instruments, sharp-edged and hard as steel, indicate the high state of civilization reached by these strange people. So interested have the scientists become that preparations are being made to equip the camp for extensive studies, and the force will be increased to thirty or forty persons.

Mr. Kinkaid was the first white child born in Idaho and has been an explorer and hunter all his life, thirty years having been in the service of the Smithsonian Institute. Even briefly recounted, his history sounds fabulous, almost grotesque.

"First, I would impress that the cavern is nearly inaccessible. The entrance is 1,486 feet down the sheer canyon wall. It is located on government land and no visitor will be allowed there under penalty of trespass. The scientists wish to work unmolested, without fear of archeological discoveries being disturbed by curio or relic hunters.

"A trip there would be fruitless, and the visitor would be sent on his way. The story of how I found the cavern has been related, but in a paragraph: I was journeying down the Colorado River in a boat, alone, looking for mineral. Some forty-two miles up the river from the El Tovar Crystal canyon, I saw on the east wall, stains in the sedimentary formation about 2,000 feet above the riverbed. There was no trail to this point, but I finally reached it with great difficulty.

"Above a shelf that hid it from view from the river, was the mouth of the cave. There are steps leading from this entrance some thirty yards to what was, at the time the cavern was inhabited, the level of the river. When I saw the chisel marks on the wall inside the entrance, I became interested, securing my gun, and went in. During that trip, I went back several hundred feet along the main passage till I came to the crypt in which I discovered the mummies. One of these I stood up and photographed by flashlight. I gathered a number of relics, which I carried down the Colorado to

Yuma, from whence I shipped them to Washington with details of the discovery. Following this, the explorations were undertaken."

The Passages

"The main passageway is about 12 feet wide, narrowing to nine feet toward the farther end. About 57 feet from the entrance, the first side-passages branch off to the right and left, along which, on both sides, are a number of rooms about the size of ordinary living rooms of today, though some are 30 by 40 feet square. These are entered by oval-shaped doors and are ventilated by round air spaces through the walls into the passages. The walls are about three feet six inches in thickness.

"The passages are chiseled or hewn as straight as could be laid out by an engineer. The ceilings of many of the rooms converge to a center. The side passages near the entrance run at a sharp angle from the main hall, but toward the rear, they gradually reach a right angle in direction."

The Shrine

"Over a hundred feet from the entrance is the cross-hall, several hundred feet long, in which are found the idol, or image, of the people's god, sitting cross-legged, with a lotus flower or lily in each hand. The cast of the face is oriental, and the carving of this cavern. The idol almost resembles Buddha, though the scientists are not certain as to what religious worship it represents. Taking into consideration everything found thus far, it is possible that this worship most resembles the ancient people of Tibet.

"Surrounding this idol are smaller images, some very beautiful in form; others crooked-necked and distorted shapes, symbolical, probably, of good and evil. There are two large cactus with protruding arms, one on each side of the dais on which the god squats. All this is carved out of hard rock resembling marble. In the opposite corner of this cross-hall were found tools of all descriptions, made of copper. These people undoubtedly knew the lost art of hardening this metal, which has been sought by chemicals for centuries without result. On a bench running around the workroom was some charcoal and other material probably used in the process. There is also slag and stuff similar to matte, showing that these ancients smelted ores, but so far no trace of where or how this was done has been discovered, nor the origin of the ore.

"Among the other finds are vases or urns and cups of copper and gold, made very artistic in design. The pottery work includes enameled ware and glazed vessels. Another passageway leads to granaries such as are found in the oriental temples. They contain seeds of various kinds. One very large storehouse has not yet been entered, as it is twelve feet high and can be reached only from above. Two copper hooks extend on the edge, which indicates that some sort of ladder was attached. These granaries are rounded, as the materials of which they are constructed, I think, is a very hard cement. A gray metal is also found in this cavern, which puzzles the scientists, for its identity has not been established. It resembles platinum. Strewn promiscuously over the floor everywhere are what people call "cats' eyes', a yellow stone of no great value. Each one is engraved with the head of the Malay type."

The Hieroglyphics

"On all the urns, or walls over doorways, and tablets of stone which were found by the image are the mysterious hieroglyphics, the key to which the Smithsonian Institute hopes yet to discover. The engraving on the tablets probably has something to do with the religion of the people. Similar hieroglyphics have been found in southern Arizona. Among the pictorial writings, only two animals are found. One is of prehistoric type."

The Crypt

"The tomb or crypt in which the mummies were found is one of the largest of the chambers, the walls slanting back at an angle of about 35 degrees. On these are tiers of mummies, each one occupying a separate hewn shelf. At the head of each is a small bench, on which is found copper cups and pieces of broken swords. Some of the mummies are covered with clay, and all are wrapped in a bark fabric.

"The urns or cups on the lower tiers are crudes, while as the higher shelves are reached, the urns are finer in design, showing a later stage of civilization. It is worthy of note that all the mummies examined so far have proved to be male, no children or females being buried here. This leads to the belief that this exterior section was the warriors' barracks.

"Among the discoveries no bones of animals have been found, no skins, no clothing, no bedding. Many of the rooms are bare but for water vessels. One room, about 40 by 700 feet, was probably the main dining hall, for cooking utensils are found here. What these people lived on is a problem, though it is presumed that they came south in the winter and farmed in the valleys, going back north in the summer.

Upwards of 50,000 people could have lived in the caverns comfortably. One theory is that the present Indian tribes found in Arizona are descendants of the serfs or slaves of the people which inhabited the cave. Undoubtedly a good many thousands of years before the Christian era, people lived here which reached a high stage of civilization. The chronology of human history is full of gaps. Professor Jordan is much enthused over the discoveries and believes that the find will prove of incalculable value in archeological work.

"One thing I have not spoken of, may be of interest. There is one chamber of the passageway to which is not ventilated, and when we approached it a deadly, snaky smell struck us. Our light would not penetrate the gloom, and until stronger ones are available we will not know what the chamber contains. Some say snakes, but other boo-hoo this idea and think it may contain a deadly gas or chemicals used by the ancients. No sounds are heard, but it smells snaky just the same. The whole underground installation gives one of shaky nerves the creeps. The gloom is like a weight on one's shoulders, and our flashlights and candles only make the darkness blacker. Imagination can revel in conjectures and ungodly daydreams back through the ages that have elapsed till the mind reels dizzily in space."

An Indian Legend

In connection with this story, it is notable that among the Hopi Indians the tradition is told that their ancestors once lived in an underworld in the Grand Canyon till dissension arose between the good and the bad, the people of one heart and the people of two hearts. Machetto, who was their chief, counseled them to leave the underworld, but there was no way out. The chief then caused a tree to grow up and pierce the roof of the underworld, and then the people of one heart climbed out. They tarried by Paisisvai (Red River), which is the Colorado, and grew grain and corn.

They sent out a message to the Temple of the Sun, asking the blessing of peace, good will and rain for people of one heart. That messenger never returned, but today at the Hopi villages at sundown can be seen the old men of the tribe out on the housetops gazing toward the sun, looking for the messenger. When he returns, their lands and ancient dwelling place will be restored to them. That is the tradition.

Among the engravings of animals in the cave is seen the image of a heart over the spot where it is located. The legend was learned by W.E. Rollins, the artist, during a year spent with the Hopi Indians.

There are two theories of the origin of the Egyptians. One is that they came from Asia; another that the racial cradle was in the upper Nile region. Heeren, an Egyptologist, believed in the Indian origin of the Egyptians. The discoveries in the Grand Canyon may throw further light on human evolution and prehistoric ages.

Now this story may seem off. It's not something you have heard about before and it's not taught in history class in school. In fact, this story was recanted and discredited shortly after this news article was written. The strange thing is, Kincaid himself told the public that his discovery was not true. He claimed that he lied about it originally. Why would he do that? He was a well-known explorer, hired by the Smithsonian. To recant his claim of the discovery would put him in the fraud category. Is it possible something more sinister happened?

Let's think about the story—a crypt, and a full unground city that thousands could have lived in for many years? Egyptian-type statues carved into the rock of the cave walls... This sounds like a great discovery. One that could possibly change the way we look at history. Maybe change history itself. Much later in time, researchers and scholars have named this cave *The Lost Egyptian City of the Grand Canyon*. Kincaid claimed the route he took was close to being impossible for someone to hike. This would definitely make it hard for anyone to find.

Does this city truly exist? If so, why has it been hidden from the public?

This is where the local history of the Grand Canyon comes into play. Who is it who has been around for generations to either confirm or deny this story? The Navajo Nation and the Hopi Indians have lived in and around the Grand Canyon for many years before Kincaid made his discovery. It's safe to say these Native Indian tribes may have some insight or at least more details.

The land where Kincaid may have found this cave is owned by the Navajo Indians. They own the land above the rim. Our government lays claims to everything below the rim. There's a possibility the Navajo Nation may know more about this story. Another possible source of information is the Hopi Indian Tribe. They've lived in the Grand Canyon area for ten thousand years. The Hopi Indian's land was a trading route hundreds of years prior to Kincaid's claims of discovering a lost city.

According to a Hopi Indian legend, an ancient people lived deep into the Grand Canyon for hundreds, if not thousands of years. The Hopi Indians state they remember a group of people who would come out of the ground to gather food and supplies. Only to disappear once again into the deep canyon. These mysterious people weren't seen very often and the Hopi Indians never made contact with this ancient culture.

Some people believe our government is covering up this story. Why would they do that? Safety is perhaps the key. If the location of the underground city were widely known, the Grand Canyon would become a dangerous place. According to Kincaid, he barely made it to the cave entrance, so it would most likely take someone with climbing skills and endurance to make the trek. Some believe the area of the lost city is a no-fly zone, and no one can get close to the entrance. Others believe the area is closed off by our military and watched 24-7 to ensure no trespassing goes on,

After several years of research, I discovered something that could be a great lead to the right person. A temporary tramway was constructed at the top ridge of the Tatahatso Point of Marble Canyon. This tramway was built in the 1950s. In 1974, a Northern Arizona University researcher took a picture of the rim above Tatahatso Point.

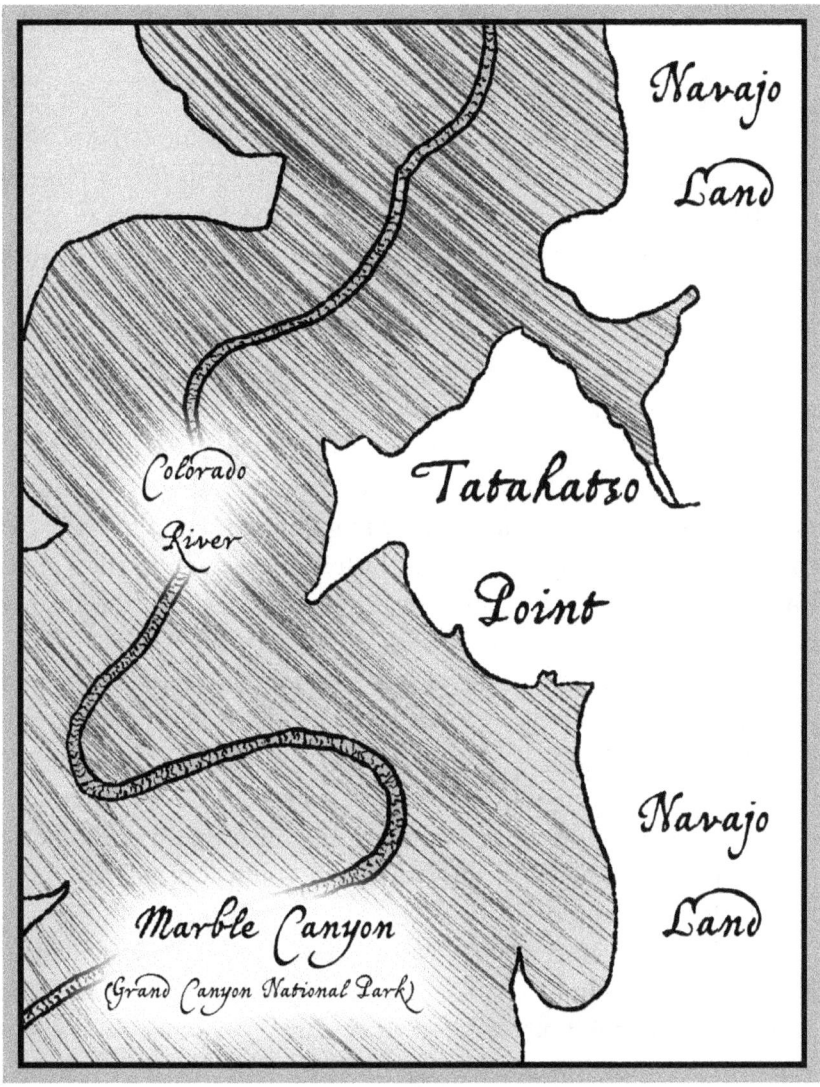

Now this area has been closed off to the public by the Navajo Nation themselves. Even in 2019, I called and made arrangements to purchase a permit to venture into this backcountry. Our team had to cancel due to other pressing business and we were not able to go and explore. Now, this area is completely closed off. The Navajo Nation owns the land from the rim of Tatahatso Point to the West. Our National Park owns the land from the cliff walls, down to the Colorado River, and across to the other side of the Grand Canyon.

This could prove to be a hard task to pursue. If the National Park isn't allowing hikers and explorers in this area, and now the Navajo Nation has closed off access to the top of Tatahatso Point, I'm not sure how any researcher and investigator could gain access.

But Tatahatso Point is almost exactly three thousand feet of rock wall from the top of the ridge to the Colorado River. This area also fits Kincaid's claim to a tee. Possibly, the tramway built in the 1950s was a way for archaeologists to reach the cave entrance to the underground city. Perhaps the artifacts have already been moved to a secret location? The truth remains to be found…maybe by you.

It would be a hard task to manage, with undoubted disappointments along the way, but it could also prove to be worth the effort. It could change the way we look at history. Egyptians in the Grand Canyon would most definitely be something new for the history books.

However, if what some people are saying is true, our government is protecting this area, so you must be careful. Clearly, you're not supposed to find it.

There are also other scholars who believe the lost city can be found in a different location, perhaps a few miles South of Tatahatso Point, or perhaps between the North and South Rim of the Grand Canyon by Isis Temple.

Another great story I came across while researching lost cities in North America is linked to the Aztecs. For thousands of years, the Aztecs lived in their homeland called Aztlan. This homeland was not where many think it is. It wasn't in Mexico where the mighty Aztecs were conquered by the early Spanish expeditions. According to Mexico's history, the Aztec culture arrived at Tenochtitlan, where they built their known city on a lake. They had the know-how and experience to build a floating island and built their structures there. The legend says the Mesoamerican tribe, Aztecs, came from the north, and there is available documentation of their voyage from Aztlan. The story goes that there were eight tribes living in the Aztlan area, each with a different purpose. Some were hunters, warriors, gatherers, builders, and more. These eight tribes made the Aztecs a powerful and prosperous civilization.

The picture above is known as the Codex Boturini, Folio 1. This document is said to show the story of how the Aztecs built their city in Mexico and traveled to their homeland Aztlan. Notice how to the right of the document, there seems to be a cave like image? Some historians in Mexico believe the homeland of the Aztecs was built underground. Just like the story of the *Lost City in the Grand Canyon*. I've been told by people who lived in Mexico that the Aztec people came from the North and they lived underground.

Here's another interesting possible clue to Aztlan where abouts may be today. Some say the Hopi Indians may have been one of the eight tribes you can see in Codex Boturini, Folio 2.

If it's true, then the Hopi Indian tribe may again have some answers to the question, could the Lost City in the Grand Canyon be Aztlan? It's definitely a possibility. But equally as possible is that Aztlan and the Lost City of the Grand Canyon are two different lost cities. Some researchers believe Aztlan was a great territory the size of several states that thrived for a couple thousand years—maybe where modern day California, Arizona, New Mexico, Texas, Nevada, Utah are today.

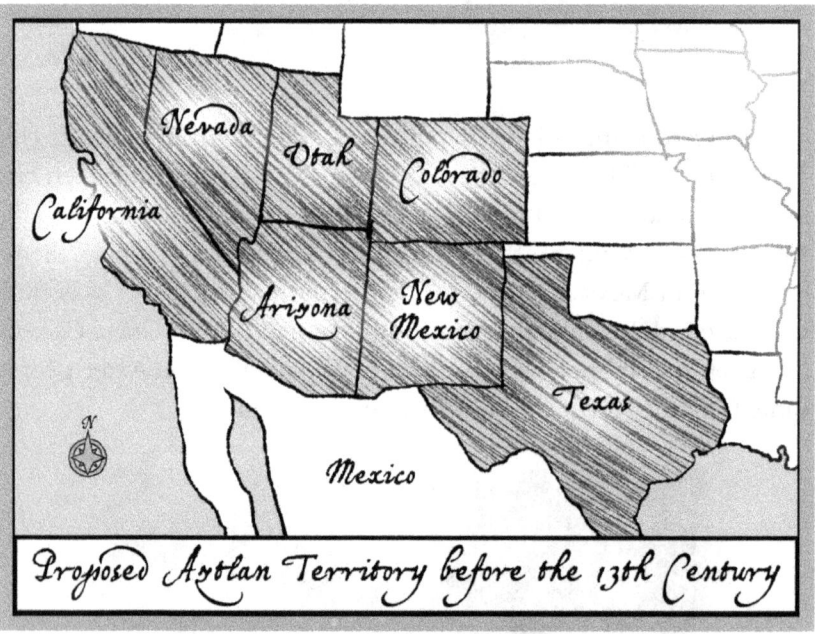

This is a big land claim. Before the United States was established, could the Southern Western states belong to the Mesoamerican people? There's many theories out there to consider and research.

For almost a year after Heran Cortes located the mighty Aztec city, he and his men stood still as they planned an attack and approach to the city. The Aztec city was a perfect designed to ward off attackers. The city was surrounded by water and was heavily guarded by warriors.

While Cortes and his men built rafts and scouted the Aztec city to learn how to attack it successfully, Montezuma ordered the city's treasures so the Spanish wouldn't find them. A group of Aztecs were said to have traveled North for months burdened by the heavy treasure to hide it in their previous homeland—which as mentioned was possibly around Kanab, Utah.

Utah has a unique past with ancient cultures. Some of its history comes from The Church of Jesus Christ of Latter Day Saints (the LDS church) and their beliefs, while more of it comes from local historians, scholars, and treasure hunters who believe Southern Utah is a filled with lost treasures.

Many people have tried to unlock the mysteries of Kanab, Utah. Since the 1800s, people have ventured into the low desert to look for the Aztec treasure. Some modern day explorers and historians have found a cave system, strange rock art, and more.

One Salt Lake City man rode his bicycle over 200 miles to arrive in Kanab. He had an old map with strange writings and symbols that pointed to the surrounding hills.

I've not seen this map, nor can I be sure it's is still around, and I certainly can't prove its existence, but at the time, the whole town of Kanab stopped their normal daily lives for months to help this man dig for treasure.

The urban legend claims the man rode into Kanab and showed his map to many of townspeople and they were convinced that there was a treasure hidden within. After some time of searching, the townspeople determined the treasure could be in what's today called Johnson Canyon. The truth and the treasure are still waiting to be found.

In the 1800s, it was common for institutions to raise money and send small groups of explorers to America to search for lost cities of gold like the *City of the Money God* and the *Lost City of Z*. This is how *Machu Picchu* and other lost cities were discovered.

Today, LiDAR-based 3D mapping technology has been used to find lost structures in Central and South America. Many new discoveries have been made in the last few years. However, even with modern day technology, many lost cities and their treasures remain shrouded in legend.

Even when a lost city is found with modern day technology, it still takes twenty-plus years to excavate the structures and have archeologists work an historical site. What happens if multiple sites are found? The logistics of the search and recovery are mindboggling.

There is still plenty to look for and discover. Between the possible cover-ups, hidden knowledge, and secret sites, treasure seekers could search America for many more generations and still not solve all the mysteries. The biggest enemy is time—will the clues to these lost sites survive, or will they be destroyed by the years, the weather, and man?

But remember, 75% of the discoveries made in modern day are made by explorers, hunters, hikers, and people who know their local history stories. There's still plenty of lost history to be discovered. You need to think logically about where to look, what you're looking for, and what equipment you need to help you be successful in your pursuit.

SEVEN

Christopher Columbus And Early Explorers

I'm going to make what might seem a bold statement. Christopher Columbus wasn't the first explorer to find America. Depending on your age, school systems have changed this part of history several times in my lifetime. Explorers have been traveling to America for hundreds of years before Christopher Columbus. There's evidence that the Chinese discovered America toward the Western States, and that the Vikings discovered the Eastern States. There's also evidence a small group of Knights Templar came to North America to hide their treasure in the 1300s, led by Henry Sinclair of Orkney. That's just naming a few different time periods and of explorers.

Due to the Internet, it's easier to find information like this. Take what you read as guidelines, not fact. Anyone with a blog, website, and social media can reach out to thousands of people. The attention and followers can seem to make a person correct and knowledgeable, but remember, they can write and say what they want. This kind of content isn't regulated and unless they have credibility, you've need to do your own research to get to the button of the story.

For example, when I was in grade school, we were told the story of Christopher Columbus trying to prove that the world was round. This was a children's story and nothing else in my opinion. Later down the road, I learned more about Christopher Columbus and his voyage. It wasn't until I went back to college and started to study history and anthropology that I learned more about this timeline. Let's take a look closer inside that story of Christopher Columbus.

Who gave Christopher Columbus the three ships to explore new lands?

Spain was the country that gave him his big break. Spain…now that's interesting because I have been studying old Spanish history for over twenty years. I can tell you there were three major countries in the world at that time who were trying to grow their empire and finances and would do anything at any cost. Spain, England, and France. All three of these countries were involved in laying claims to land in America. All three played a role in discovering new lands, growing crops, finding riches, and conquering native civilizations. All three countries were involved in the pirate ages. They also played a role in early American wars and battles. Out of the three, I can think of one that stood out the most.

One country did more damage than we could ever imagine. Spain was the deadliest culture to land in America. They conquered the Incas. They defeated the Aztecs. They laid claim where modern day Mexico City is, and used that as their new world headquarters for over 300 years. Spain carried some of the heaviest loaded ships from Mexico's ports to Spain's ports. These ships were carrying precious valuables like silver, gold, gems, and pearls. They also carried spices, sugar, tobacco, silk, and more. All of this type of cargo would have not only bettered their country, but it would have also been good for their economy by trading and selling to other countries. This is business and it's why Spain became forceful and deadly to ancient cultures in America.

Is it possible Spain had a bigger plan? Did Spain hear of early explorers before them finding resources and ancient cities made of gold and follow up to chase riches and prosperity?

I strongly believe Spain knew of the possibilities in the new world and they wanted to be the first to find out if the stories were true. Times were different then. The ancient civilizations that were killed and erased from history had their cultures and languages lost forever. Spain claims it was done for God and Glory, but I only see greed and spilt blood. Cultures were conquered and forced to live the way of the Spanish. They were taught the Spanish language and forced to give up their religions and turn to Catholicism. The Mayan population became nearly extinct in the 1600s.

After time, these civilizations grew and prospered again, but it was at a very high cost. I'm guessing Central and South Americans would have different lives today if Spain hadn't shown up in the past.

This wasn't the only effect Spain had on the Americas. Later, after Spain settled into Mexico, the Spanish traveled to what's known as North America today. There they took Native Americas (Indians) as slaves and worked many mines for gold and silver. Many local Indian tribes people were killed. The expected life span of a Spanish slave working the mines was three months to a year. There's a reason why the native Indians weren't too agreeable to becoming a part of the United States in the 1800s and 1900s—they had already had their fair share of white man troubles.

It was 1421, when China discovered America. An author named Gavin Menzies wrote his first book about this voyage. He wrote a

15,000-page book explaining what history he discovered. This would be a great book for you to read if you would like to learn more about the history of China and the new world.

Let's go back in time about four hundred years. There has been new evidence uncovered about a Viking fleet of ships that entered into the boundaries of America in the 10th century, when the Viking explorer, Leif Erikson, sailed to a new land. Many believe that this new land was modern day North America.

It does sound reasonable due to the fact the Vikings did explore nearby continents like Greenland and Iceland. If you spend a few minutes looking at a world map or globe, it's easy to see why the Vikings may have traveled a little more South and discovered the shores of Nova Scotia and more. Some believe that the Vikings may have sailed as far as Michigan, Wisconsin, and Indiana. Some believe that in the 10th century, the St. Lawrence River was wider and easy to sail a Viking ship from the North Atlantic Ocean to the St. Lawrence River. That would have led them to where modern day city Chicago is today and the surrounding lands. Some say from there, the Vikings even traveled into Newfoundland and Canada as well. Even though this is not proven or recognized by all professionals, this is another story that you can research for yourself.

A farmer found what is known as the Kensington Runestone in 1898. He was discredited from the start but he swore until the day he died that he found the stone of Viking symbols in his field. If there's one thing that I can accomplish by writing this book, it would be to open your mind to accept new found historical information. It will make you a good explorer and the possibilities are endless if you use lost history correctly and efficiently. Now let's move ahead to the date 1398. Henry Sinclair of the Knights Templar did sail out to sea. At this time, I can tell you that the Knights Templar were still in hiding from France. King Phillip the IV killed many of the Knights Templar in 1307. This is where Friday the 13th comes into play. On October 13th, 1307, King Phillip burned many Knights

If you didn't know this part of history, I bet you will never think of Friday the 13th the same again. Because of this tragic situation, many thought the Knights Templar order was gone and broken forever. This is not true. There were still many Knights Templar and loyalists that were not killed on the 13th and many of them went into hiding. The Holy Grail and the Templars' treasure was still lost and many people believe that the Templars kept the location secret until they could move it to a new location. History and evidence shows that some noble families from Scotland allowed the last Templars to hide in their castles. Many believe in hidden underground tunnels and rooms. There has been evidence that shows Templar symbols underground in some Scottish castles. The Sinclair family name is one of them. I know this because Henry Sinclair of Oakley was my 17th great grandfather. My family tree has been revealed and the Sinclairs were in our bloodline for over 400 years from 1000 A.D. to 1500 A.D. These records have been found by myself after taking a DNA test back in 2015. Around that time, I spent more than a year researching my family tree and collecting as many old documents as possible.

Many of the Sinclairs were crusaders and were trusted by the Templars. In fact, that's how Henry Sinclair became the leader of the voyage to find new land, generations of Sinclairs proved themselves to be loyal to God and the Templars. There's evidence that the Templars were able to get several ships and stock to pile up their treasure to take to a new and far away land. Henry Sinclair heard from some fisherman that had accidentally found new land during a storm. This storm pushed their ships in the wrong direction and they stumbled onto new land that they have not seen before. When Henry Sinclair heard of this story he found the fisherman and asked them if they could find the land again. A deal was struck and not long later, the Templars sailed to America with a few loaded shops believed to be the treasure of the Knights Templar.

As you can see, there are many accounts of explorers finding America before Christopher Columbus. I think this is very important because as a treasure explorer would say, knowing this information means that even more possible treasures could be recovered in North America. Expand your mind and do a little research. If your budget is slim, explore and research history in your hometown. I guarantee you that your life will be more fulfilled by exploring nature. The fresh air and beautiful scenery is one of the treasures in search.

I've never come home empty-handed before. Even when I didn't find a lost mine or buried relics, I have the memories of a lifetime. I've seen so much in my field research and my health is better because of it, both mental and physical.

EIGHT

Early Spanish Exploration

This section of my book is going to really help you if you have an interest in Old Spanish history in America and/or if you live in an area that is known for Spanish explorations. The Spanish had 3 main ports connected to North America, and because of their locations, it served the Spanish well to explore many of the Southern states. That being said I'm always learning new ports that the Spanish used. There were many but I'm going to focus on the top 3 to paint a picture for you. Because the headquarters of the Spanish was in Mexico City, it's safe to say that if you lived in the Western states, you most likely could find lost Spanish history and possibly treasures.

    States like California, Arizona, New Mexico, Utah, Nevada, and Colorado. Throughout the years, many people from Idaho, Oregon, Washington, Wyoming, and even Montana have reached out to me and mentioned they believe the Spanish traveled that far North in pursuit of mining for minerals. I can believe that. I haven't been able to confirm the Northern states yet but I've been shown pictures of rock, structures of old mining features, and more and it does look like a time period and is correct to Spanish origin. I know from history that when the Incas and Aztecs were conquered, the Spanish learned about more cities of wealth and they traveled in Arizona very quickly. From what I've researched, as early as the mid-1500s, the Spanish were traveling in and out of Arizona and New Mexico looking for their next targets.

Many people believe that the Spanish started to explore Utah shortly after as well. I know that there are many treasure hunters in New Mexico that would tell you they've found many mines and buried treasures in their state, too. Nevada has many stories from local Indians claiming there was an Old Spanish trail through their state. There's one thing to keep in mind about the wild west: it was ungoverned and unclaimed for many, many years. This gave ample opportunity to the Spanish because no one but local native tribes could stop them. Some western states didn't become part of the United States until the 1800s. Utah wasn't considered part of the United States until 1896. As you can see and imagine, the Spanish had free rein over this territory from around 1521 into the late 1800s. That's almost 300 years of conquering, mining, and development in America.

That could possibly be the longest time any outsider had the chance to rule the lands of Mexico and North America. People ask me all the time why I believe there's still lost treasure in the United States, and now I'm going to go more into depth on why I believe there's still hundreds, if not thousands of lost treasures, relics, structures, lost mines, and buried treasure in North America.

Let's go to the next port, Florida. This was a very popular port. It was the first stop from Spain and the gateway to the Caribbean Sea. For many years the Spanish built forts and other structures in Florida and surrounding states. This led to one of the reasons why the Spanish gained a stronghold in America. There were ports further to the North as well. States like Georgia and South Carolina had several missions.

This was a thriving area for the Spanish and If I lived in the area, I would be searching for anything to do with the Spanish. The possibilities could be endless. Another popular place that I recently learned of is Texas. This state has another stronghold in this area. Many missions and forts were built. San Antonio would be one of the first places I would start looking. There was a Spanish port South of San Antonio and that created a perfect path inland to Texas. If you live in the Southern states of the United States, you could make a great discovery. I'm going to list states below so you can really see the impact the Spanish made on this land.

As I mentioned earlier in this chapter, there are states to the North that the Spanish explored as well. Those states in the table graph above are the most commonly known states but Spanish occupation/exploitation was not limited to only them. It's the western states that served mining and precious minerals for the Spanish. The eastern states provided land, cities, and their strongholds. When it comes to treasure hunting there's two different categories. Treasure hunters that look for treasures on land and treasure hunters that look in the sea. Both categories make for extensive searching. I'm going to be honest, I don't live in the eastern states and my research has been 80 percent in the western states. So I'm going to go more into details of what I know and leave the eastern states to those experts and professionals when it comes to Spanish explorations.

I can tell you that there's great scholars, treasure hunters, explorers, and historians in the Eastern states and if you want to learn more you need to start making relations in these areas. Start by doing web searches. Read books from local authors in your area. Reach out to some of these people. Our team does have two contacts in the Eastern States. Marc Hoover is a part of our team and a good friend of mine. He lives in Florida. My father, Craig Draper lives in South Carolina. They would most likely enjoy hearing from you if you're interested. We all know that the Spanish did conquer the Inca empire in Peru. It's easy to find history of the Spanish explorations in that area. I would suggest the same for you if you live in those parts of America, reach out to experts in your area. There's rich history there and I guarantee you will find plenty of lost history. If I were you, I would start looking for ancient lost cities. I know I have but we'll save that information for another time. Perhaps another book. Again I have not spent a lot of time in that area. I've done a lot of research and our team is gearing up to explore Central and South America in the next few years.

My research is extensive in the Western states so let's go from there. After discovering and conquering the Aztecs, the Spanish made a headquarters right in the center of where Mexico City is today. This was a main city and port. Most of the written records of the Spanish in the field ended up in Mexico City and then those records and documents were sent to the King of Spain on ships. We have learned in the last few years that many documents and maps were copied and saved in archives in Mexico City and the originals were sent to Spain. Mexico City has proven to be a great resource for researchers. Many documents still are kept in Mexico and not just in protected libraries and museums. We've discovered that old buildings that served as record buildings, missions, churches, and more have old records in the basements and other areas of the buildings. These documents are starting to decay and grow old enough that some can't be unfolded due to the document being destroyed.

In the right hands, someone could possibly become very educated in the realm of the Spanish. Treasure maps, Waybills, and more could be found and if you have these types of documents, you could find yourself closer to a treasure than you could ever imagine. Treasure hunters and historians have been finding old documents for hundreds of years now. I've seen old Spanish maps and documents and held them in my own hands. Some of them are sold as a collector's prize. Some of them have been traded or sold from treasure hunter to treasure hunter. These old maps and documents do exist, so don't discard that possibility from your research and exploring. The cost would not be cheap but it could be well worth it. I know that many hunters have acquired old maps and documents at the cost of five hundred dollars, all the way to ten thousand dollars for each map and document.

I mentioned the word "waybill" earlier. You may have asked, "What is a waybill?" The Spanish used this name to explain a document that was written by a representative of a person of power. The writer had knowledge in the written language and understood the dialogue and terminology. This was ever important to have a writer in every group that ventured in the wilderness for the Spanish. The waybill was meant to be read by leaders in Mexico and to be sent to the King of Spain. A waybill had many purposes. Mainly to make the leaders and the King of Spain aware of significant findings or events. For example, if a group of Spaniards were in New Mexico exploring the terrain and found a rich vein of silver and gold, this type of news was recorded in Mexico City. The waybill would explain a general area of where the minerals were found and what the group of Spanish was doing with the minerals. It would also go into details of if they started a mine and how large it was. It would also explain how pure the minerals were. There would also be a plan in motion described as well. How long they'd been mining. How much gold and silver they have recovered and how much more they plan on finding. It would give reports of the Commander's name, and how many people were in their group.

If there were hostile Indians in the area, that would have been mentioned as well. A waybill was a professional document that gave very important information to the leaders and King. These Waybill documents would have been saved and protected for many years to come. All were filled and saved. The King of Spain would sometimes go through old waybills and send a group out to rework and reclaim mines, recover a treasure left behind, and much more. If you find a waybill, you most likely would have plenty of information, approximate location to the important event in time, and discoveries.

Waybills were also used to explain a situation where the Spanish buried and left a treasure. Usually their treasure was rich mines, gold, and silver. Think of a waybill as an important document to explain anything of importance. Old Spanish maps are another important document that was created by an appointed Spaniard. The map maker had to have knowledge in distance used by the Spanish. Vara's were a popular measurement that can be found on maps, tree symbols, and rock symbols. These maps, like the waybill, were created by a professional and were sent to Mexico City for their records and then to the King of Spain. Some old treasure maps were drawn to show a wide-range map to mines and treasure. Some large maps may show you several miles of the landscape. Some maps were created to show only a couple of miles.

Another thing about maps is sometimes there are more than one. Sometimes if an area of interest to the Spanish was large, they would create one large map and sometimes they would create a few maps, showing different areas of a large landscape. Sometimes a Spanish Captain would have the Waybill creator and the map maker work together and send both to Mexico at the same time. Sometimes a Waybill was sent and a couple years later, a map was sent. There is no exact way to do it. These documents served as a way of telling news of important things.

If you ever have a chance to see or acquire one of these two or both, you should consider it. Even if it's not from your area. Make sure you do the legwork to make sure the document is authentic. This could prove a little hard at the time but if you can find someone that can tell the difference between old paper used in the old days from the current days, that can help. If you can find an expert that knows the language, that will be a bonus, too. Old Spanish writing is different from new Spanish. Even a paper written by an Hispanic in the 1950s would be different from the writings of a Spaniard in the 1700s. The wording and terminology would be different and even confusing.

Now, you may be asking yourself, what kind of things should I look for when it comes to Spanish treasures in North America? Let's go into some scenarios and explanations of these types of treasures. The first thing to understand is things of value. Early in this book I mentioned the things that are of value to the Spanish. Gold, silver, gems, pearls, silk, sugar, tobacco, and more. From my research, lost mines are prime sites to make discoveries. Lost cities are the same as well. The Spanish was always on the lookout to make new discoveries of these valuable things. Sites where they mined, are ground zero. If you can find a location where they mined, then you could stumble on possible caches hidden in the area of silver and gold bars, virgin mining ore, relics, artifacts, massacre sites, grave sites, structures, smelters, arrastras, and so much more. These mine sites may have been worked for 20 plus years. Sometimes even longer.

Depending on the purity of the gold and silver, including how much virgin material was available would set the pace of the work conducted in the area. If a gold and silver vein was high in quality and was a large deposit, they wouldn't leave until the minerals were no longer available or until something or someone made them abandon the area. If the mine only produced a little amount of minerals, then they would abandon the area and start to look for more areas. This is why the Spanish spent so much time in the Western states.

Why was the Spanish mining more in the Western states of North America?

It's because of one important thing. Mineral deposits of large amounts have always proven to be more and in higher grade form in the West to the East. You've heard of the old Gold Rush era? The states were California, Nevada, Arizona, Utah, Colorado, Alaska, and more. You can't create gold and silver out of nothing. If you start to create a mine, it doesn't mean you will find minerals. You've to be at the right places and dig to the correct depths. The Spanish were experts and some of their mining methods are lost with time. They knew what they were doing and just like the map makers and document writers, they had geologists and mining experts in every Spanish group. These types of expeditions were not by accident, they were well planned and thought out. If a group of Spaniards accidently stumbled onto a new discovery and they didn't have the equipment, man-power and know-how, they would have written to Mexico and asked for those experts. Their system was large and dedicated.

Of course there was more that the Spanish focused on but the mining and finding lost cities, and rich civilizations were key to the Spanish. Here's some information that may help you understand even more. The Spanish didn't always start mining from scratch. What I mean by that is there's many records, documents, and spoken/written history of the Spanish finding rich ancient mines that were not played-out. In Central and South America, the Spanish wrote reports on finding old mines from the Incas, Mayans, and Aztecs after they conquered their lands. Due to explorations conducted by the Spanish once an area was deemed theirs, they would expand and explore for more resources.

Some of these reports went into great details of these old ancient mines, dug by others before them. I know and I've been able to confirm this, if a rich old mine tunnel or shaft was discovered, the Spanish would investigate it. If experts said that there's still minerals to be dug-out, then the Spanish would continue on from where others left off. Studies and reports from myself, mentors, and colleagues have all agreed on this subject. The way we discovered this was old documents reporting the discoveries of the Spanish but always scientific test to date the timbers and diggings done by the Spanish. One mine alone that I can think of that I've worked and studied in an area, proved to be older than the time that Spanish started mining it. According to the documents, the Spanish started to mine in 1719. My mentor found the mine in the 1980s. Him and his partner noticed that the mine had different timbers (mine props) within the mine. A few years down the road, they decided to test the mine props. What the test results showed was the mine timbers were much older than the early 1700s. In fact, the test results showed that some of the mine timbers were made of a tree species that no longer live on the mountains and shows that the timbers were most likely cut and placed in the mine in the 12th century.

We all know that the Spanish weren't there that early. So who dugout the mine before them? This isn't the first time that this type of situation has been brought to my attention. Groups from Arizona and New Mexico have spoken to me about the same thing at one of their discovered mine sites. This led me to believe that the Spanish were chasing stories hundreds of years ago. We have many reports of the Spanish landing in America, speaking to people in villages, gaining knowledge of successful civilizations, and tracing their whereabouts. I truly believe this to be true. This is why I mention research and talk to people that have family and friends that have lived in the area of interest for many generations. Those types of stories bring some truth and some meat on the bones.

So I know you have questions on who dug the mines before the Spanish? This is not a fact and my team will continue investigating this topic for many more years I'm sure. Some people have claimed that it was the Aztecs. Some have claims that it was the Maya, and even the Incas. Perhaps that could be true. I do know that the Aztecs had the Mixtec culture make many of their fine gold jewelry and artifacts because the Mixtec were experts in gold workings. Maybe it could be them. When the Spanish conquered the land of Central and South America, there were many old mine diggings in that area. This is a topic that I will not go much more into due to lack of evidence. I will say that some of you that read this book may have some ideas. I think this should be looked into further so that the history of mining can be updated. Someone was mining a lot in North America before Spanish.

Let's head to a different section of this chapter. Let's talk about lost cities and why they played a big role in why the Spanish move in curtain patterns and dedication of the globe. Searching for lost cities of gold and riches has been a dream of many for thousands of years. Because America was a new world and new lands to explore. Many cultures and people traveled to America for hundreds of years. We've all heard of Eldorado. This is a story that has been told and dreamed of by many around the world. Stories like this are what kept the Spanish moving forward. Lost mines, virgin gold and silver, silk, tobacco, and more were just a bonus to the Spanish. The lost cities of gold were not out of the Spaniards' scope. They seem to be gold and silver, gems and robes, silk, and more from the cities of the Incas and Aztecs. These stories of lost, rich cities were thought up to the Spanish a lot. They had a reason to believe that more civilizations may have richer cities than the Aztecs and Incas. The Spanish had a way to that landed them new information. Mostly of fear, many cultures would point to a mountain range and tell the Spanish that there's richer people living there.

I have reports that many smaller cultures heard of the wrath of the Spanish and that they would say anything to turn the Spanish attention to a faraway place from them. Many reports from Hernan Cortes and Francisco Coronado were written about their explorations. In these reports, you can learn what they were looking for. Their list is as follows but not limited to. The Lost 7 Cities of Gold, the Lost City of Z, the Lost City of the Monkey God, and many more. These same reports were later discovered by the British and other countries from Europe. That's when discovering lost cities in America became so popular in the 1800s and 1900s.

Percy Fawcett was a great example of an explorer who believed lost cities and riches could still be found in the new world (America). Percy spent much of his life looking for lost cities. He felt his home in Europe several times to map the Amazon Jungle. Some say that he was only there to create maps of South America but when you look into his life, you can see that he learned of many mysteries and lost civilizations that needed further investigations. Unfortunately, he very much returned home but during his expedition, he claimed to have made a great discovery. He is known for the Lost City of Z. He was never seen again in 1925. That wasn't that long ago when you really think of time. In 1925 people were still mapping unexplored areas and I can tell you from my research, these are still many areas in America that are unexplored. I have reports that Central and South America have territories that have not been explored in modern days. Places like Honduras and Brazil have areas that are off limits and protected by its government to protect indigenous cultures. Many of these indigenous cultures still live today as their ancestors did. Some of them do not know of our modern day world. They know nothing about big cities made of concrete and technology.

This gives you an idea of what's still available to explore in America. In these unknown places, only the locals that still live there know about the terrain. I have heard that some of these cultures stay away from certain areas. They claim that their people know of lost ruins, overgrown in the forest that had thousands of people living there in the past. Do you know that the Lost City of the Monkey God, also known as the City of the Jaguar, was just discovered in 2014? A team wasn't able to research the location until 2017. A small team of archaeologists, anthropologists, and more ventured to the location found by LIDAR and found statues, artifacts, and even buried structures. The country of Honduras is working on uncovering the city but they claim that once it's founded and approved, it would still take 20 to 30 years to uncover its mysteries.

This is how I know that many discoveries will still be found for many years to come. In the professional world, one site like the City of the Jaguar will take many resources and money to conduct their field research. Many sites today are delayed for many years and there's only so many professionals that are interested in taking on these types of discoveries. Thinking of these older discoveries and all the new discoveries to come, I know that's why people and early explorers have entered into America before Christopher Columbus. Reports and documents of ancient civilizations and ruins have been reported for hundreds of years.

If you work hard and research, you could be the next famous person in history to make a great discovery. It takes time and persistence. Don't let that stop you from doing something you feel you truly should do. Local people, scholars, and outdoorsmen have made up to 70% of the new world's discovery. That's right. The common people have found most of the major and important discoveries. Then they report to the right people and if it's possible, the professionals will follow later on.

NINE

Transporting Treasure From Land To Sea

The goal of exploring the new world was to make new discoveries to either bring back valuables to their home country or bring news of discoveries of the new world. The Spanish spent over 300 years bringing back treasures to Spain. This chapter will explain how they did that and why there's still lost treasures on land and in the sea.

If you want to understand how and where to look for lost history and treasures, you need to understand the history of transporting cargo to and from. The Spanish didn't only take from America, they also brought new things to America. Reports and history show that the Spanish brought horses, cattle, chickens, goats, pigs, and more to America. This changed things as we know it in America. This was a huge operation conducted by the Spanish. They intended on making America their new lands and many things were taken and brought to and from Spain and America. For example, the Spanish tore down much of the Aztecs structures in Mexico City. Then, they built their missions and city. Spain claimed the land and started using the resources to the best of their ability.

Exports and documents show that the Spanish traveled in every direction from their capital in Mexico. They traveled to explore and gain knowledge of minerals, civilizations, water sources, building materials. This is just an example of the operations conducted during their time in America. When it comes to treasures and other valuable things, the Spanish took their riches seriously. Like I mentioned in some of the previous chapters, it sometimes took months to years to explore America. Using horses helped and made traveling faster but in most cases, they could only travel up to 50 miles in a day, if the horses are not loaded heavily with gear. If the Spanish traveled with their gear, it could have slowed them down to 15 to 30 miles a day.

It also depended on water sources, the terrain, and the endurance of the horse. It's safe to say that travel was slow and they didn't want to waste resources and manpower. Especially when it came to gold, silver, silk, spices, and more. I'm going to give you an example of what it was like to transport treasure from one location to another.

Here's a disclaimer for the following: this section is a fictional story, based on true events and historical research to help explain the mining process and events to get the treasure to a ship for Spain.

The Spanish found a rich source of silver veins in the high mountains, south of Santa Fe New Mexico. They waste no time rounding up workers and slaves to open mines. Some Spaniards collect slaves, some start preparing to build mining structures like Spanish arrastras and Spanish smelters within the mining area. Others write to their headquarters in Mexico City to ask for mules, horses, tools, and more. After a year, the Spanish successfully opened 3 mine tunnels in a remote area of the mountains. [1] Their smelters have been melting down silver bars and store them in a nearby cave opening with a wooden door built at the entrance. At this time, they have manufactured 30 bars of silver, 5 bars of gold, and 50 bars of copper.

The mining camp is thriving and over 20 Spaniards take charge of delegating the workload to their slaves. Hunting parties are on the move to feed everyone every day and scouts separate to stand guard to protect their mines from any possible thieves. The geologist of the group wonders the nearby area to scout for more virgin silver veins.

One year and six months later, the King of Spain requests a report of the minerals retrieved from the mines. The Spanish party writes back to the King to explain that the mines are still producing silver and other minerals and the stockpile is growing every month. In this report, which could also be claimed as a waybill, the Spanish party explains that the silver bars should be transported to Mexico City before next winter. Once Mexico gets the reports, they send more men to move the treasure, mules, horses, tools so the mining group can continue their process for minerals. It takes this incoming party of Spaniards all round a month and a half of trekking to arrive at the location of the mining group.

After several days of resting the traveling Spaniards and horses, they spend 5 days gathering and packing the ore, silver, gold, and copper bars on mules and begin their descent down the high mountains and towards their way to Mexico City. During this trek, the Spanish could only travel around 15 miles a day due to the heavy load carried by the mules. They have to make many stops for resting and hunting. Every time they stop the mule train, they have to look for food sources and water. Keep in mind that this happen at least once a day, if not more.

This is a very important part of survival. During this time, the Spanish had their fair share of hostile Indians and outlaws trying to claim the treasure for themselves. The Spanish were successful in winning every battle because their men were heavily armed with guns and swords. A few of the Spanish men have been killed which caused the party to travel even slower. [2] After a little over 4 months of travel, the Spanish party arrives in Mexico City. The treasure is intact and they pass it on to another group to prepare the minerals to board one of their ships at the port.

Mexico City takes the virgin ore and smelts it down at the local smelters. Preparers take inventory of the valuables for the ship's manifest so records are ready once it arrives in Spain. [3] Once the Spanish ship leaves Mexico, a different group of sailors live the long and hard life at sea. The Spanish ship sees a few pirate ships along the way and changes their course from the normal route to avoid conflict or battles. After 2 months of sailing, the ship arrives at the Port of Spain. The King of Spain takes another victory as the ship is unloaded. The ship's manifest details show that the ship was loaded from many different gathering and mining groups like the one I explain above. Spain prospered and continued this way of life until the late 1800s.

Understanding the events of the Spanish is very important if you want to look for lost history and treasure in America. What I explained above is only one story of thousands and thousands. I also told a story of success and victory, not failed missions. In my research, I found that more missions like this one failed more often than succeeded. What happened to the treasures and the Spaniards belongings? This is where treasure hunting comes into play.

Consider this, the same story happened but the ship heading to Spain was attacked by the English at sea. Both ships are still floating in the ocean but the English take over the Spanish ship at sea and relocate the Spanish contents to their ship. Imagine now that the English ship is sailing to London, heavily burdened by the treasure. Now the king of England is the winner and they prosper. That's one scenario. I could come up with many scenarios but I'm going to change the story a little three more times. Again, keep in mind this story is fictional but based on true events and historical records and events.

In the above story, you'll notice a number after a paragraph[#]. These are the next segments or storylines I would like to explain to you. These stories are based on my research and events that I've found as real events that have happened many times, in different areas, during different time periods. Let's start with segment [1] and go in order from there.

In segment [1], the Spanish open 3 silver mines and their mining process has been a victory. Every winter, the Spanish prepare their camp and abandon it until the spring comes. Year after year this occurs. Indian slaves' life span would only last from 6 months to a year. Some

Spanish groups would venture into the area and enter Indian camps to gather slaves but it wasn't always a fight at first.

The Spanish found a new tribe of natives and decided to befriend them to learn more about their people, culture, and the history of the area. After a couple weeks, the Spanish had traded with the native tribe and set up camp only a short distance away so they could stay in communication frequently. The Spanish asked the chief one day if he had ever seen or heard of gold and silver in the area. The chief wasn't sure what they were talking about so the Spanish pulled a few small gold nuggets and silver out of their pockets. The chief recognized the minerals right away and pointed to a nearby mountain range that the Spanish hadn't explored yet. That night seemed to be the same as the other nights until native warriors heard the screams from their women.

The Spanish came into their camp, after dark, and started to take all the healthy men from the camp. They used rope to tie the natives hand and made them kneel on the ground. Many native warriors took up their weapons to fight the Spanish but unfortunately, the Spanish killed off most of the threatening natives. By sunset, the natives camp was nothing but smoke from the fires set to the natives' teepees. The natives' dogs laid on the ground dead and the Spanish only spared the old men and women. The Spanish also gathered women as well. They needed them for cooking, gatherings, and running the arrastras. After a few days of travel, the new Indian slaves found themselves in the high mountains. Once they reached the Spanish mining camp, they saw many other Indians that were working. Very quickly the new Indians were divided and put to work. Some worked in the mine tunnels and some worked in the surrounding area conducting other tasks. Winters and summers have come and gone. The mines were dug very deep into the ground and the Spanish were developing a lot of minerals.

One night, the Indians are waking up to gunshots and screaming from wounded Spaniards. The battle continued for hours until the night became quiet. The Indian slaves laid quiet, not knowing what to expect. Soon after a few minutes, the slaves hear a familiar language. They got on their feet to see that many Spaniards were lying in a pool of blood. The Indians wasted no time. Some of them started to dig deep and big holes at the campsite. Some of them collected tools and belongings of the Spaniards and once the holes were completed, the Indians threw the Spaniards belongings in the hole. The Spaniards bodies were dragged and thrown in the hole as well. The other Indians were placing the Spaniards tools and leftover belongings in the mines.

This event took place in many areas and sites that I've discovered and explored. The Indians didn't keep the gold and silver. They wanted to leave it where mother earth extended it to be. The minerals had no value to the Indians. It wasn't worth anything to them. All the Indians knew is that white men were evil and they only wanted to ease their existence forever. These types of sites were never visited by the Indians again. Sometimes the medicine man would curse the land. Sometimes, new Spaniards would return to the mining area to look for their missing people. Only to find small traces and patterns of other Spanish once existing in the area. Sometimes, the Indians would keep a close eye on the area and if any other Spaniards entered the mountains, they would kill them and bury them too. If it was a small group of Spaniards, the Indians wouldn't dig graves. Out of disrespect for the Spaniards, they might leave their bodies to rot.

I have found more sites similar to the above story than any other during my field research and exploring. You can see why this area would be of interest to other historians and treasure hunters. The Indians didn't get rid of the clues left behind from the Spanish. They left their smelters, arrastras, tree carvings, and more where they were. This makes it to where a trained hunter can come in the area, even 250 years later and find clues and evidence that the Spanish were in the area. The Indians would always find all the Spaniards belongings either. There's been some reports of Spanish swords, armor, and more having been found behind for a lucky person to find.

The mines, sometimes are harder to find, and then again, sometimes not. In the past, I've found the structures and artifacts from the Spanish but not the mines. Sometimes I've come across an old mine opening that appears to be somewhat hidden but erosion after time has opened part of the entrance. Not one site is the same. You need to keep an eye out for everything that doesn't seem natural. Let's go to another scenario in this story so you can see that the treasure may not be at the mine site, it could be on the trail. Let's go back to the part of the story where I explain the Spanish on the trail, making their way to Mexico City.

In segment, the Spanish have been traveling for a couple months now. They're growing weaker every day and water is hard to find in the desert. After a few days, the Spanish find a watering hole and decide to camp for a few days. Within 2 days of rest, a local Indian scout saw the Spanish in the distance. The Indian scout returns to his camp to tell the tribes chief what he saw. The tribe has heard of the Spaniards way of life and by that night, they decide they're going to defeat the Spanish party. Early in the morning, the Spanish awoke, only to see that Indians were standing over them with weapons. Within a matter of a few minutes, the Spanish were all killed. This Indian tribe didn't bury the Spanish. They didn't hide anything in a hole. They decided to leave the bodies and their belongings where they laid.

The Indians did take their time to go through the Spaniards' belongings. Anything that was deemed worthy, was taken. The Spaniards' horses and mules were gathered up and prepared to travel. The Indians didn't take the ore bags of gold and silver and throw them into the water hole. Hoping the minerals would never be seen again. After three days of the massacre, four trappers hunting in the area found the Spanish rotting bodies on the ground. They knew it was due to the Indians because the dead men had arrows in their bodies and horse tracks that lead to the South. They didn't find the gold and silver but they carefully examined the bodies and found weapons, a map, and a waybill. The trappers decided to leave the area due to fear of the hostile Indians.

Six months later, the trappers returned to their homes and the trappers told their family members what they found. Two out of four trappers kept the Spaniards belongings and the story was pasted down for a couple generations. Even 150 years later, the area is known for a legend of a battle between the Spanish and the Indians.

There's another treasure for you. The gold and silver may still be in the water. Perhaps the water is dried up and now the gold and silver rest 12 inches in the ground. Not to mention the waybill and map. The family passed those down to friends they knew that wanted to try their luck at treasure hunting. In recent days, that map has been sold to several locals, hoping to find the treasure. Call it what you want but I can tell you these are based on real events that have been discovered and/or evidence of the treasure still lost today. You can see how this is playing out. You have to think out of the box. Everything you know of the modern world is different than the old days. Especially in the Wild West. The West was the last frontier. Most of the states in the west were not inhabited by Americans until the late 1800s.

Many stories and legends have been written and passed down over the centuries. You may be surprised by what you find in your states if you do some research and talk with the right people. I believe if you're determined enough, you can be on your way. I spent the first couple years learning from treasure hunting books and local history of what might be in my area. Sometimes I found legends and stories quickly and sometimes I had to research for many months. Getting to know your area is key and remember, not all stories, historical accounts, and legends are real. Sometimes they have a little truth to them. Sometimes they're completely wrong or lies, and sometimes the locations are wrong after generations. Let's go to the last segment of this storyline. We have stayed on land to explain where treasures may be found. Now let's go to the sea.

In segment [3], find the part where the Spanish had loaded their ship full of valuables. The Spanish ship made its way from the port of Mexico, heading to the Gulf of Mexico and then to the Caribbean

Sea. South of Jamaica, the sailing crew sees that bad weather is coming their way. The Captain decides to veer off course a lot, hoping that they will miss the storm. By that night, the storm hit the ship very hard. The waves were hitting the ship and pushing it towards the North. The Captain can't see but tries to navigate through it. A few sailors have been thrown overboard due to the waves and many of the men are scared for their lives. Within four hours of fighting the storm, the crew member noticed land ahead. The ship was moving far too fast for the Captain to turn the ship away and the ship crashed into the land mass. By morning, only a couple crew members made it to shore. From land, they look back at the crash site to see that most of the ship is not intact. Many floating objects were seen by the survivors and their whereabouts were unknown. The few crew members start traveling on foot to find some help.

When they arrived in a small village, they couldn't speak the natives' language. Their story wasn't explained to the village people but they did help them with their wounds, feed them, and gave them shelter for some time. These survivors never made it back to their homes in Spain. Many ships were sent out to find the missing ship but nothing was ever discovered. Spain spent the next 4 months looking for possible wreckage but they were unsuccessful with that as well.

Somewhere between Jamaica and Haiti, a sunken treasure lays at the bottom of the ocean. It would take advanced divers and scouters to find the treasure. If someone can figure out the location, they would find everything that the sea has not deteriorated. This is why I say, never pass up an opportunity to hunt your area. I can't imagine that we know of all the treasure sites that are lost. It may be several generations later until someone makes a small discovery of the records that this ship is still lost and its whereabouts. I want you to remember and consider that this was only one story of lost treasures and mines. I created a total of four different scenarios from one event to another. I have researched and archived over a hundred stories of possible legends with treasures in the West. Every month, my files grow with new possibilities, stories, and sites.

TEN

Sunken Ships In The Caribbean

If you like the sea, pirates, and treasure, you're going to like this chapter. I decided to include this section in this book because I think it's very important to know what type of treasure you want to hunt for. If you like the history of sailing at sea, you're going to enjoy it. We all have seen movies of pirates and Black Beard, now you can understand the behind the scenes of life at sea. I'm going to bring up the Spanish War between Spain and England, then I'll move to the era of pirates and how that came to play with treasure and riches. I explained a little about the Spanish and transporting their cargo from Mexico City to Spain but I didn't get into the history of hundreds of years of different countries fighting over the riches.

One thing to understand is for thousands of years, one civilization has been conquering other civilizations for power, land, and riches. This has been a way of life most likely since the beginning of man. Biblical stories mention this as well. Everywhere you research, you'll find that type of behavior. For many years in my research I thought it was more of a territory situation, but then I understood the reasoning. Money. Power and money have been a big factor in wars. It can start off with a different motivation but at the end, it's power. Without money you can't have power. Both go hand in hand.

I do know that some cultures like the Vikings looked at it as a way of life.

They wanted new lands to grow crops and live their life. Once they conquered a civilization, money and treasure were found almost every time. The treasure they gathered over the years gave them the ability to travel and look for more land. This is the way it's been for a very long time. Skipping ahead a few hundred years to the mid-1500s, the Spanish have been successful in bringing heavily loaded ships back and forth from the New World to Spain. This gained attention from other powerful countries like England and France. One word got out of the Spanish success, things began to head in a new direction. It was obvious that the Spanish empire was growing fast and becoming more and more powerful.

Spain's economy grew dramatically. With their new growth in wealth, the King of Spain was able to build more ships, pay for more troops so he could expand his army. The King of Spain set in place troops not only on the water, but on land in neighboring countries. This made Spain a stronghold and ensured that venues will continue to flow in their country. Spain expanded their cargo by bringing crops from the new world. This didn't only benefit their country. Spain traded goods with many other countries which in turn, brought more income to their economy. England and France were still a force to be reckoned with at that time.

Rumors of war and other tactics were starting to spread. By the later 1500s, some battles started to take place and even though Spain laid claim to all sunken treasures from their ships, England and France started to do a little of their own treasure hunting.

By sailing the seas looking for Spanish wreckage, England, and other countries, was able to see that Spain was growing very powerful. The Spanish War (some call it World War Zero) started in 1585 between Spain and England. England wasn't new to war and had a very powerful Navy, which in turn proved good for them. England had many warships. These English ships were large and could carry more cannons then most naval ships of its time. These ships would carry hundreds of men which was necessary due to the manpower that was needed to operate the artillery. England won many victories and in turn Spain started to build faster ships with more cannons. Battles during this war were hard. Some ships were faster than others and if a ship had more men and cannons, the slower it could sail.

Some ships were able to outrun other ships and in reality, war ships would have to be fairly close in the proximity of the other ship, in order to successfully fire their cannons and hit their targets accurately. As Spain started the construction of new ships, England contracted privateers founded by private money. This was a way to grow their emperor with even more war ships. England didn't have to build new ships, they simply bought the Captain, crew, and ship. These privateers had the Crown of England official license to track and hunt down Spanish ships. This license was known as the "Letter of Marque." This will give you an idea on how many privateer ships where after the Spanish and their cargo, 1,622 letters of marque were given to these private ships.

That's over 1600 private war ships, out on the hunt to track down and rob Spanish Ships. Under the letter of marque from the King of England, these privateers had the right and used it to their advantage to rob Spanish ships and take the treasure and valuables for themselves. You can imagine that these private ships were on a mission to wealth. According to England, it was legal to do so. Many educated and known men took up privateering for the purpose of striking it rich. This created chaos in the Caribbean Sea and the Spanish grew weaker and power as the time went on. History doesn't tell many stories of what the privateers did with their money. It's hard to say how much was lost and stolen but one thing is for sure, many treasures were lost at sea and even buried on the shores. The Spanish War continued for twelve years. The war did hurt England and Spain financially. The war had to come to an end because plain and simple, England and Spain couldn't afford to continue the way they did.

In 1604, the win was declared to England, without a doubt. Even then the war came to a halt very quickly and some claim that England and Spain were both broke, or close to that. Both sides agreed to stop the war. At this time, it was clear to both sides that things were only going to get worse. Even though England and Spain had peace, there were a few groups that weren't taking the immediate loss of work and money to their liking. Many ships stopped and popular ports were overcrowded. It was no longer legal to attack the Spanish ships. Even though Spain and England tried to lick their wounds and move on to other business, the privateers were laid off and now finding themselves restless and running out of money. The English Navy downsized from about 50,000 sailors to 13,000. Thousands of people were hurting for money and the privateers were wasting their money at ports, drinking and having their fun with prostitutes. This was a huge unemployment time in history. Not only were the privateers out of work, over seventy percent of the English Navy was too. There was no work and only the fortunate were able to financially take care of their families.

The biggest problem, further than unemployment, was many of the nonworking sailors were trained fighters and learned to rob after 12 years of free range war and plundering. Not all the men agreed with the stop of the war and in many cases, these men should be feared if they can't find a new way of living. After some time, these sailors started to come up with their own ideas on how to make money. After some time, the Spanish moved back to their riches in America. Ships were starting to move again and valuables were arriving in Spain. The King of Spain contracted privateers to work for the Spanish. Their job was to protect the heavy Spanish ships from coast to coast. These privateers were known to be some of the worst kind of privateers. More cutthroat than the English privateers. Even though England and Spain signed their peace treaty, the Spanish privateers were still attacking some English ships and taking the variables from English ships.

Word started to spread around from port to port to the laid off English privateers and they didn't take to the news very well. The King of English ordered for all his past privateers to stand down and not retaliate against the Spanish. Months went by and even a couple years later while the Spanish weren't practicing peace against England. This didn't go well with some of the laid off English privateers. Talk about the Spanish betrayals and plundering was a common conversation among some. Some of the privateers went to the English lords in the Caribbean ports, only to be told that the King of England wanted them to stand down and not do anything. After some time, a couple of known privateer ships and crews disappeared in the Caribbean Sea and they made their way up the Eastern Coast to ports that didn't have a strong English hold. This is where the tide turns and privateering changes.

Going against the Kings of England's wishes, private ships started to secretly attack Spanish ships. This caused a ripple in the Caribbean due to many England loyalists being scared of what the King of England may do and how the Spanish might retaliate. Fear was growing fast on the Eastern coast of North America. The small groups of private ships started to do more than make a little money robbing Spanish ships. Some ships started to become feared and well-known. By the 1700s, the people of the New World started to call the self-appointed privateers pirates and the attacks and plundering started to grow more intensely. This is the era of Black Beard and many more. Going against the grain was no longer and concern of the privates and wealth and greed was feeling their souls. The plundering continues and the battles became more wicked and vile. Pirate ships started to grow in numbers. Captains and crews were multiplying. Some of the well-known pirates were very successful in taking Spanish ships in battles and grew very wealthy. Some were so wealthy that many stories of private ships sailing to uninhabitable coastlines to hide treasure on the shore were growing.

Sometimes when a Spanish ship was conquered and plundered, the private ships were too small to take on the burden of its new cargo. This caused many private ships to sail slowly and even take on water, forcing them to land their ship at a beach to bury their treasure. News spread of possible treasures buried on coastlines, islands, and shores and that only brought even more greedy men and new pirates. This was the time of the Pirate Republic, so they called themselves and as they grew stronger and wealthy, so did their ships. Many of the successful private crews decided that they needed bigger and faster ships. Ship with more guns and the capability to carry larger crews. The unemployment rate started to shrink in the

New World and many had to choose what side they wanted to be on. Many England loyalists stayed in the allegiants of England, staying far away from pirate activities.

Some of the islands and the English loyalists had no choice in the matter. Some privates started to call their homes where English people lived. Ports like Tortuga, Nassau, Port Royal were overrun by pirates. Many private ships could be found docked at their ports. The Spanish did start to retaliate against the pirates by contracting even more privateers in their fleets that wouldn't take prisoners. The pirates could be fearless but the Spanish privateers were just as evil, sometimes seven more. This fueled some known private Captains like Black Beard and created a hostile environment for many at sea. Treasures were taken and lost at sea. Some of the treasures were under the water as some laid at a beach, waiting to be discovered. Even though the pirates intended to come back for their stolen treasures, many pirates never made it back to recover them.

Some were killed at sea and some had to give up the pirate's life for good. Some claim that private history started in the 1600s and carried on until the 1800s. That may be true but for the most part, pirates were stopped by England starting in the late 1700s. The King of England organized British crews to track down and hunt pirates. Some pirates lost their lives and some were given the option to sign a stop pirating contract. The contracts signed were between England and the individual private themselves stating they would return home and discontinue their ways of privateering. By the 1800s, North America was growing stronger at this time and England no longer had a stronghold on the land, nor did Spain. The United States of America took the matter into their own hands and pirates as we have all seen in Hollywood movies came to a stop.

I only summarized a little about the history of pirates, the Spanish, and the English. When people ask me why I believe pirate treasures are still lost today, this history comes to my mind. Just imagine all the ships that were lost at sea during this time. Battles were lost and won and many ships were blown to pieces at the bottom of the sea. Many treasures that were hidden on lonely islands and are still lost due to the lack of records. When it comes to this era of history, anything can be possible. Never assume that all the treasures have been found. Let's take the Florida coast for example. You can find that many discoveries have been made in the last 100 years. From experienced treasure hunting ships with permits, all the way to metal detectorists have found artifacts and sunken ships off the coast. It's hard to pull a permit to look for sunken ships in today's time. It's not only costly, some countries like Spain and England still lay claims to these lost ships in the Atlantic today. These countries claim that even though it's been a couple hundred years since the ship has sunk, it's still their property. This makes it hard to legally claim a new discovery today.

I have many friends that are in the world of seeking lost sunken ships and I heard about new discoveries now and then. I've also been able to work with filming producers and major networks that claim it's almost impossible to get permits to film these lost wreckage ship sites. I always working with a major network in 2021 that told me that our plans had to change and that we needed to choose another story inland because of the problems that came with filming the lost ship sites. Politics and regulations are hard to get past and I fear for many more years to come, places like Florida will have to wait to make discoveries. The same goes for shipwrecks in and around the coast of Mexico. It's still up in the air how they should be able to claim the treasures of the sunken ships.

Should its riches go to Mexico because it's their shores or should Spain be able to claim them because it was originally theirs?

The Spanish may have even wrongfully plundered the treasure from native cultures in Mexico that is lost at sea.

Should Spain be able to keep those riches if a person discovered a Spanish ship off the coast?

There are the questions that come with hunting and discovering riches and lost treasures in the ocean. I've heard of recovery ships like Odyssey that have recently discovered a new shipwreck and within a matter of a couple weeks, planes from Spain can be seen, spying on the recovery ships activities. When that happens, news comes to magazines and newspapers and everyone can hear about the discovery. Take in account that the public only knows around

10% of what is going on in the world of discoveries. Our media and higher power determines what to show and share with the public. This way it can be contained and controlled. If sunken treasures are your cup of tea, I would like to invite you to look into the history of the normal routes used by the Spanish and the records of where some of these lost ships lay in the ocean today. This could be the start of your treasure map to sunken treasure and artifacts.

Some lucky people in our present time have found artifacts on the beach with metal detectors. Some have accidentally found and made discoveries while on the beach, on a family trip. I don't care what the newspapers say. Us treasure hunters share reports of our discoveries and they happen a lot more than you know. Most treasure hunters don't share their discoveries with the rest of the world. Because of this, many outsiders don't realize the progress that is happening in the world of historical researchers, treasure hunters, and scholars today. This is why I mention early in this book that one key factory plays in your future if you want to join this world of treasure hunting, find knowledgeable friends that have been doing this for many years. There're many good people in the world of treasure hunting. The public has painted them as grave robbers and historical thieves but I know better than that. There's good and bad people in every group of society today. Most of the time, a few create a bad name for many.

Using history is key to get you started on your journey. This is a great starting point. By researching what shipwrecks have been found in your area and by tracing the routes of these ships, you'll be closer to becoming a treasure hunter. Here's one thing to remember. Commercial planes fly in a route pattern. These routes don't change. The only thing that changes is the way you approach the landing and how you take off. Once in flight you keep to the course. This route and regulations keep the planes on course and if anything was to happen to the plane, its tracks can be traced. The Spanish, English, and many more have sailed their ships the same way. Merchant ships and more have done the same. These Spanish ships that sailed from Spain to America stayed on the path. Only in time of need did that Capitan change course. A couple reasons were if they hit a bad storm or if they were being chased by pirates or privateers.

Even if a ship changed its course, it would go back to the original course plan once it was clear of danger. This was a great design so the rightful country could send rescue ships out to look for the lost ship. History and records show that some were found and recovered. You can find records of rescue ships that reported not only finding the lost ship a couple months later, sometimes they were able to send word that they need more ships to bring back its cargo and sometimes the ship's crew. Not all lost ships have been permanently lost. Spain has good records and so does Mexico City. If you have the right connections or if you work in the field of some professionals, you could get a chance to see some of these records. Many of them sit in protected areas and buildings of Spain today.

There have been a lucky few that have seen these records, translated them, and released them into the public. Doing some searching online can get you headed in the right direction as well. If you learn the routes, you can narrow down the area's. Keep a close eye on shallow waters. Captains were aware of the shallow waters but sometimes bad weather and high winds would push the ship towards the shallow water. This is where possible shipwrecks could still be. I've done this too but don't expect to find the shipwreck on Google Earth. Chances are slim to none because these old ships were made of wood. Everything on a ship decays with water and time. Even the iron used on ships will deteriorate after time. One of the only metals you can depend on finding (not using satellite imaging) would be gold, silver, copper, and more.

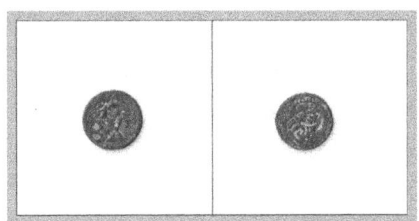

Bronze Coin Found by Author (dating back to the Fifteenth Century)

Keep in mind that a single Spanish gold coin found could land you thousands of dollars. Especially if you can link the coin, or any artifact, to a ship's name. I've seen them go for more than fifty-thousand dollars and more. Who says treasure hunting can't pay off? That could be a great find and I know many people who would do almost anything to make a discovery like that.

Hopefully, just from my pictures from this book alone, you can see that discoveries are made and will continue to be made if we do our due diligence of research. Later in this book, you will find many more pictures of artifacts, symbols carved in trees and rock, structures and much more. I'll make a believer out of you yet. I've only gotten started on the path of treasure hunting.

Now back to treasures lost at sea. Do not get discouraged because you're not finding what you want right away. I will warn you that treasure hunting in itself is time consuming on land or water. When it comes to sunken ships, it could prove even more difficult and expensive. If you already have a boat and live close to the shore, you can surpass many hunters. Most people only dream of hunting for sunken shipwrecks for a vacation type trip, once in their lives. You could already have the upper hand. Now the tricky part is scuba diving. If you want to find treasure at sea, you will need to have a diver. If you're not fit to do this, you can always get a diver or two or three in your group. This is somewhat of a timely thing to get your certification and be on your way. It's not as hard as you think. Some people are made to scuba dive and enjoy it very much while others struggle with breathing oxygen in the water with a mask. This is something you will have to learn for yourself. The equipment is another cost but manageable. Everything costs money when it comes to treasure hunting.

Another thing is the depth of water.

A master diver can only go so deep in the water. The pressure is so great that you should never go more than a hundred and fifty feet deep. Even if you can get your master divers certification and conduct a deep sea dive like the one I'm explaining, you will have to keep in mind that you can't just dive that deep and come back out of the water. Depending on the elevation, you will have to descend and ascend in small increments. Diving deep, or surfacing too quickly can result in The Bends., also known as decompression sickness. This is a deadly thing that can happen and will result in death if not treated properly right away. You will do all this by taking your driver's test and classes. Do your homework and see if this type of activity seems to fit you.

If I was you, I would reach out to some metal detectorists in the area you want to hunt. Make some friends and ask around if people have been or have ever found ship artifacts in the area. If you can't find anyone to help you with information, one of your first plans should be to buy a beach metal detector and do some scouting on your own. By doing this you can see for yourself if you can find artifacts on the beach. If you do, there's a good chance that a sunken ship is in the area just waiting to be discovered. There's many beach detectors on the market made by many brands.

ELEVEN

Using Lost History To Find Locations

It's time to start to learn how to use correct history to find your treasures. Beginning with known history is key, but this chapter will help you learn how to take several sets forward in learning the right history, History that can point you to the right mountain range or section of the sea. This technique has proven worthy for myself and my mentors before me.

Spanish Arrastra Found by Author in Southern Utah

Take this Spanish arrastra for example. Local history tells a story of copper miners from the 1800s who built this for crushing down minerals to make bricks for a kiln in the area for mining. I took the word of the person paid by the state of Utah to determine and examine this structure. I revisited this site for several years after seeing it for the first time. After getting to know the area and field researching, I discovered the Spanish mined two extremely rich silver mines very nearby. After finding many clues in the area, I came to the conclusion there's a possibility this altar was built by the Spanish, not local Utah miners in the 1800s. Let me explain more about how I separated local history from what I researched in the field.

In 2011, I started my research in Southern Utah after moving there a year prior. At the time, I was attending Dixie University for anthropology and history, along with my general education classes. I spent a lot of time at school, taking 12 to15 credits per semester, but when I wasn't studying, I spent a lot of my time wandering the high mountains. I had a lot of fun hiking and exploring, but I missed the known places and treasure sites I was familiar with in Northern Utah and Western Idaho. I was used to chasing after sites people passed down by word of mouth, books, and local history, but Southern Utah was a new area. After a year of exploring, I wasn't finding evidence of any lost history, structures, or clues in the field. I started researching on the web where forums were beginning to become popular. After spending a couple months searching the web, I realized I was about ten miles too far to the west.

I read forums where locals talked about the Mountain Meadows Massacre site and some lost mines, which were not too far from there. I decided to head out to the east, and from there, things started to change for me. Within a couple months, I found a very old and large ponderosa pine tree with some strange markings carved into it. I went home and found help to determine if the carvings in the tree were old. A friend of mine got back to me after I emailed him the pics of the carvings. The response I received was exactly what I was looking for. He told me the symbols appeared a couple of hundred years old based on the bark. He also told me the symbols resemble similar Spanish markings that usually point to a mine or possible treasure.

He asked me to go back and take more pictures of the three carvings on the tree. He asked me to take different angles of the markings so he could see them better. A few months later, he traveled south to meet me and see the markings himself. After twenty minutes of examining the markings, he gave me a big smile and said, "you may have found very old Spanish symbols, possibly dating back to the 1700s."

I asked him how he knew that from the markings. He then showed me how to field the age of the carvings by using a large carpenter square. He placed the carpenter square on the tree itself and measured the distance from the bark, to the trunk of the tree, inside the carvings itself.

The symbols were about two and a half to three inches deep. Which means the carvings may have been just under 300 years old. I was shocked and amazed. I then had him explain the process a couple more times so I could remember how to conduct a field test on my own in the future.

He also told me that he uses lichen in the and around the carving to compare the depth of the carving to the age of the lichen. Again both tests came back around three hundred years old. I had found my first possible evidence that the Spanish were in southern Utah about 300 years ago. One of the symbols definitely looked like a marking the Spanish used for a mine. The other two symbols were so overgrown by the bark of the trees to make out the exact nature of the marking. Those symbols will have to wait until I can find a better way to retrieve the information left behind.

My friend went home the following day, but he told me that he would go to his files to see if he had any further information and/or stories from the same area. A few days later, he emailed me with a story researched by himself and a friend. Both of them visited the area back in the 1980s and interviewed a couple old ranchers. The ranchers told them that their families owned land nearby for over 100 years.

The ranchers had a couple stories that aligned with my symbol tree. The email went on to mention that one rancher found an old structure about four miles north of my tree symbols. The old rancher didn't recognize the building methods or the purpose of the structure itself. The rancher mentioned that part of the rock structure was crumbling down on one end. After my friend drew the rancher a picture, the rancher agreed that the structure may have looked similar to a Spanish smelter.

Now I had two pieces of evidence pointing to the Spanish in the area.

I spent another year, exploring the area like a grid. Every time I covered an area, I mapped it and recorded the GPS coordinates so I could keep track of what I had learned in the field.

After a second year, I began to see a pattern on my map. It showed a possible trail and direction traveled by the Spanish. I knew I had to find the smelter described by the rancher, so my friend and I met with the local Indian tribe. They told us there was a story passed down by many generations from their tribe that told of the Spanish coming to the area and discovering a rich silver vein, causing them to dig two mines near where I had found the tree symbols. I was further excited three months later when I actually found the structure the old rancher had described.

Spanish Smelter Found by the Author in 2012

I couldn't believe I'd found it. One end was crumbled down as described. When examined, it proved to be the doorway into the smelter. The discovery of the smelter proved someone had been mining in the area. From reading the lichen, it appeared the structure was possibly 250 years old.

This is just a field test and not exact science but it's a rough date. After further investigation, we found that inside the smelter, there was evidence that the smelter was used. You can still see today how the inside got so hot, it started melting the individual rocks together. This was a perfect discovery. Now I wanted to use this story as an example that you can't just take history as the way it's told. Nothing of Utah's history talked about the Spanish in the area, at any time. The clues and evidence I found in the field did go along with the local tribes' story. In this case I can tell you that you are the investigator. If you're finding evidence that doesn't go along with your local history, dig into it. Put that history to the test and see what you come up with. There's more to this story but I'm going to save that for another time, book, or video documentary. The bottom line is, I don't believe that the arrastra shown at the beginning of this chapter was built in the late 1800s by the copper miners. Arrastras were used by the Spanish to crush down ore with silver in it. It's not used for gold, copper, or any other minerals. It's an old method of extracting the silver from the hard rock and has been used in Europe for a very long time now. Hundreds, if not thousands of years.

Unless the copper miners in the late 1880s knew of the Spaniards method and design, it wasn't built by anyone other than the Spanish. This also goes along with what the local tribe told us. Two rich silver mines in the area. I will say that I reached out to the local archeologist and anthropologist and I was told over the phone he following:

"What you found is interesting but it can't be Spanish. The Spanish never traveled this far north. It may be from Native Americans or early settlers from the 1850s to the early 1900s."

Did you hear that? The professionals in the western states do not believe the Spanish came to Utah or any other states further than Arizona and New Mexico. I dare you to do a Google search to see how many legends and stories have been passed down about the Spanish coming to Utah in the 1600s to mine for gold, silver, copper, and other minerals. You will be surprised what you find. It is not just Utah, Nevada, Idaho, Wyoming and other neighboring states. It goes back to my experiences in this same area. I also found rock monuments that resembled very similar to Spanish built rock monuments. The list goes on from there. I found horseshoes with a metal detector near the Spanish smelter. When I dug them out of the ground, about 7" deep in the soil, I noticed that not only did they look old, they were very thin and appeared to be made in the field.

When I returned home, I pondered on the horseshoes for a couple weeks until I decided to find a local man that was an expert on horses. I took one of the horseshoes to this expert and he did examine this. Within a few minutes, he commented on how thin they were. We wondered if it was because of the material they were made of which was iron but, I believe something else was in play. He went on to tell me that the only time horsemen would use thin horseshoes in the modern day period would be for parades. He went on to say that if you want the horse to stand out, thin horseshoes would make the horse trot. This way the horse would look more impressive. When he told me that, I remember stories of the Spanish coming into Central America in the early 1500s. Local people in that area still have tales of the shiny men of large animals with metal weapons. The local people talked about how they had never seen these animals or men until then and they thought they were gods.

For hundreds of years after that, the Spanish would do all they could to look more powerful and intimidating. That's when I relived that the Spanish were and still are today known as horse experts. For hundreds and hundreds of years, the Spanish have had some of the best horses in the world. I think it would be very feasible that the Spanish did understand how to make horses and themselves appear more intimidating. I think I found 3 horseshoes from the Spanish, dating from the 1700s, and these were other clues to unlocking the mystery of this lost history in the area. I can't prove this at this point. These are only my observations, based on what I've seen and discovered of this area.

If there's anything I can do to help you understand a little more about it, is the history we all know and were taught. I can't speak for history that I've not researched but I can speak up for many stories of lost history in the Western States. I can guarantee you that I could take you out within a day and you would see what I mean.

Old Rock Monuments Found by Author

I have more information on my discoveries in this remote area that I would like to share with you. I could write another book about it but I'm going to stop at this point. I can tell you that on my websites, there's more to read. I can also tell you that I have a web series out that you can watch, it's called "Uncharted Expedition". In Season 1, episodes 2 and 3, my team and I venture into this area once again, only this time on camera. In these two episodes, you can see more of this area and the new discoveries we found, documented in our archives and transferred to the web series.

Let's move onto another story in this chapter so you can see that all of history is told correctly. In fact, sometimes people lie and deceive others so they can hide the truth, or their wrong doing and faults. This next section is about one of the worst massacres, still to this day, that has ever happened on North America's soil. Some say that it's one of the worst crimes ever committed in the history of

America. For some of you, this story might hit you at home. Others of you may have heard of this story from a different perspective. Some of you have been lied to for over one hundred and sixty years. On the Old Spanish Trail, also known as the California Road, there is green meadow with clear water flowing to the south. This area for many years had served its purpose for resting to many travelers. This was a great stopping point after a hard journey. Today it is known as the Mountain Meadows Massacre of Utah.

Trappers, Spanish parties, and travelers alike knew of this place. It was one of the most common places to stop on the trail, due to the harsh environment from the south. I have read reports and journals that talk about this place. Some travelers would stop and rest for weeks at this location to hunt for food and to rest and water their horses. This was an unfortunate experience for a large group of Arkansas people known as the Baker-Francher party. In the early part of the year in 1857, the Baker party formed a wagon train of many families. They weren't all Arkansas people. Some other parties joined the Arkansas people to travel West, to their destination in southern California. Most of these families sold their homes, businesses, and took all their belongings with them to start a new life in a new location.

This was a hard road and life to live in those days. Just like the story you have heard of the Old Oregon Trail. History says that 120 people belonged to this wagon trail but after doing a report of my own, I learned that that was only the known people. I conducted a new article with a few local news channels and asked several people to get involved. I discovered that there were some hired hands that were not accounted for. I think this party was more in the 140 - 150 people that belonged to the Baker Party, including everyone. This wagon train had a huge mixture of people young and old. The Baker Party didn't sell everything they owned before leaving Arkansas. History shows that some of the families were known for extremely high breeds of horses and cows.

Some of these animals were worse than others and one thing is a fact, these prize animals were some of the most sought-out horses and cows that ever entered into Utah state.

We're not talking about ten or twenty horses and cows, I'm talking about hundreds and hundreds of heads of cattle and horses. Possibly thousands.

The Author, Interviewed at Mountain Meadows for a local Newspaper in Southern Utah

It is unfortunate that the Baker Party was able to travel fairly safely, through many states until they entered into Northern Utah where the modern city of Salt Lake City is today. When the Baker Party visited the City of Salt Lake, conflict started to rise and many verbal arguments started to happen between the local Utah people and the Baker Party. Utah is known for many things and one thing is for The Church of Jesus Christ of Latter Day Saints, also known as Mormons and/or LDS.

You see in the past, the LDS church didn't always have a great name for themselves, according to outsiders of their church. The LDS people came from the East, where their church was originally formed. Not all Easterners agreed with the LDS church's methods and values. Let's say this, the LDS church started a branch in Arkansas in the earlier part of the 1800s and not all Arkansas people wanted them there. Needless to say, these two very different groups didn't see eye to eye and tension started to grow in Utah. Word started to spread as the Baker Party traveled south in Utah. At one point, the Baker Party needed supplies and stopped in a town of Utah, only to be refused services and goods. The Baker Party was very large and needed supplies for the rest of their journey and after being turned away, unkind words were passed back and forth between the parties. After some conflicts and not so friendly words exchanged between the two groups, the Baker Party left town, low on supplies and morale, frustrated and angry at Utah people. Same went for the Utah people. Utah continued to receive letters from Salt Lake City, suggesting that the Baker Party should be refused goods.

By the time the Baker Party reached the Southern part of Utah at Mountain Meadows, rest and food was an essential part of surviving. The Baker Party found exactly what everyone before found in Mountain Meadows, a lush green meadow with crystal clear water and food to hunt to feed their people. A few days went by and the Baker family was still in Mountain Meadows resting and gathering natural resources. Letters were still written and passed back between the Utah residence. These letters were from Salt Lake City, asking about the Baker Parties activities and whereabouts. Southern Utah people wrote back explaining that the Baker Party had set up a large camp at Mountain Meadows and were still there after many days. A couple days later, orders for the North were given to keep a close eye on the Arkansas people.

After about a week and a half, Utah residences grew tired of the Baker Party and scouts were set to watch them. At this point, the Utah residence decided to do something about the, what was looked at, unwelcome party, trespassing people. At one point, the first battle happened. The Baker Party quickly circled the wagons in the meadow, trying to protect their families and group. Utah history says that many battles were conducted over four days but I like to say five days. One of the battles was later explained to be an attack by the local Paiute Indians against the Baker Party. I don't believe they were Paiutes. I believe that it was Utah residents trying to blame the attacks on the Paiutes.

I have done extensive research on this story and area and nothing but the Utah residences claim, shows that the Paiutes were ever involved. Sadly, after the five days of battle during the night and day, the Baker Party was running out of water and food, ammo and the endurance to keep fighting. The Baker Party was surrounded and Utah was winning. At one point, the Baker Party surrendered, putting their guns down and standing together with white flags and their hands in the air. The Utah residences did capture the Baker Party and separated them in groups. One group were boys and men while the other was girls and women. The groups were marched, separated north through the meadow, one further ahead than the other. The furthest group was the females and what they heard next must have been a horrible, tragic thing.

Mountain Meadows Monument, Built in 1999

As the females were walking with some of their hands still in the air and some holding their small children, the sound of guns being fired echoed through the land. Not just one. Not a few shots but many. The females heard the cries of their sons, fathers, grandfathers, and friends. Once the screams stopped the meadow was quiet, the Baker Party females started to run, only to have the same to them. Only a handful of small children were spared. History tells that a few children under the age of 7 were kept alive. A monument is one of the only things that stand in Mountain Meadows today. This monument was built in the year 1999. Decayed bones were found during this time of the Baker Party while concrete pathways and dirt trails were built.

Before I go on with the rest of my story, I would like to mention that my heart, sympathy, and devotion goes to the Baker Party and their families. I have been involved with the modern day history of the Mountain Meadows Massacre from 2011 to the present day. I'm still leaning in the Baker Party's favor and that's due to my research, evidence I've discovered over the years, and due to my moral values. I will not stop investigating this site until I can't do it anymore.

This story was one that I contemplated on during the time of writing this book. I love Utah for many reasons but when it comes to its dark past like this story, I stand down and follow my instincts. I would like to also mention that times were different back in the 1800s. People were different and mistakes were made. I just wish this one wasn't part of Utah's history.

The reason I decided to write about this story is because I feel that it's important to tell history the way it is and that it's important to understand the truth. If you visit Mountain Meadows today, you will find many plaques that explain in brief details what happened with this massacre. I have read them all before I started investigating this site. I want you to know that these plaques and the land where the monument stands today, is on land that is owned by the LDS church. This is not government land, BLM, or Forest Service.

This is private land and the location of the monument and what is said on the plaques are done and written by the LDS church. That leads me to the reason for using this story as an example of using history to find locations. Not all history is correct, honest, or even intended for the greater good. It's sometimes used to beat around the bush and even draw attention away from a certain group, country, and/or organization. Let's go more into details and my intent of this story so you can understand what I mean. After the massacre happened at Mountain Meadows, the United States government was made aware of this tragic event. At the time, Utah was not a part of the United States of America. The U.S. Cavalry rode North to the meadows and found dead bodies lying on the ground and wreckage of the Baker Parties belonging. The cavalry built a monument in the middle of the field and buried the bodies. They also cleaned up the area and tried to put it back the way it was.

During this time, the cavalry was also on a mission to find out what happened and who was involved. After a little time, the finger was pointed at the local Paiute Indian tribe and the cavalry noticed that the site didn't appear to be a normal death site of an Indian attack. Arrows were not stuck in the bodies and the traditional ways of Indian soldiers did not seem to be present in the field. The cavalry started to look at the local Utah residences for answers and after some investigation, the cavalry caught their murders. It was discovered that members of the LDS were to blame for the vicious attack on the Baker Party. This is one of these points where someone needs to go to jail and take the blame. Because the U.S. laws didn't exist in Utah at the time, the cavalry had a hard time using their force.

Several months later a man named John D. Lee was put in jail for the murders of the Baker Party. Found what I researched, Utah wasn't allowing anyone else to take the fall, only one man that happened to be related to the LDS church leader, Brigham Young. John D. Lee was later sentenced to death by a firing squad and in Utah's eyes, the man was sentenced and he now paid for his crime. During the time that John D. Lee was in jail, he left a clue that could change the way history tells of the Mountain Meadows Massacre.

He drew a map of Mountain Meadows that showed the massacre location. Along this map, it shows the route that the Baker Party marched in and has a few more clues. This is where I come into play with the modern day research of this event. I was given this map from my mentor, many years ago. I was told that it was a treasure map, leading to a cache of guns, and belonging to the Baker Party. I didn't spend any time looking for the treasure. I've always been more in tuned to the history of the massacre. Local newspapers started to reach out to me, asking if I would get involved with a new article and discoveries of the area. I expected. The first news article that came out, they explained my involvement as a treasure hunter that knew of the history. After that article went live, I started to get a lot of people reaching out to me.

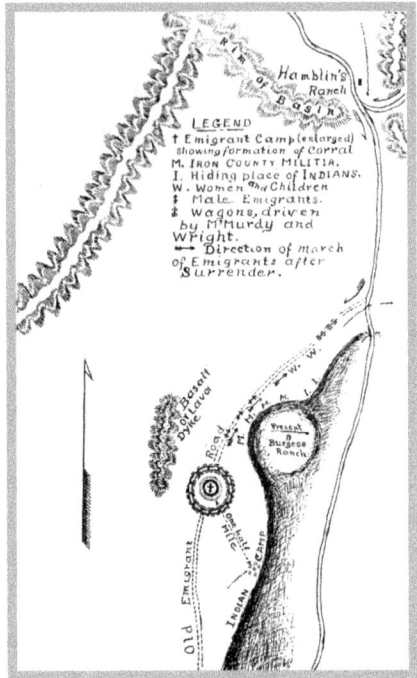

Map of Mountain Meadows, Utah in the western United States

Surprisingly, some of these new contacts were neither neighboring landowners from LDS church property. A few of them mentioned that their families involved reached deep during the time of the Massacre and that they would like to present some thighs to me. I accepted without hesitation and agreed to meet them at the modern day massacre site. What I learned next was almost as shocking as the history of the massacre itself. I'm not going to go too much into details, I'm only going to summarize this next part, just like I've done so far. To be blunt, there are still a lot of bad feelings between the LDS church and the present family members of the Baker Party. To the surviving family members, the story of Mountain Meadows Massacre still isn't resolved and they want the truth to be told. They also have the right to tell the story as they see fit and with the monument and being on LDS land, they can't do that.

So a land battle and dispute is still going on today. The Baker Party family members want to create their own monument. Write their own plaques, and the story as they like. I have seen the confidential court papers, explaining that the monument is built in the right spot of the meadows. Legal battles are taking place so the Baker Party families can do as they feel is right. This has been years and years in the work. I was shown an old, crumbed down rock monument that sits a couple miles to the North East from where the present monument stands today. This old rock pile appears to be an old cemetery maker. The landowner that showed it to me and my wife, told me that this was the real, original location of the men that were killed in the Baker Party. But there's a catch. This old monument is not on LDS land, it's just a little off by a few acres. It sits on a man's family lot that has been theirs since the massacre.

This is where the legal battle comes into play. If it can be proved by the Baker Party families in court, the surviving family members may have a chance to purchase or lease the ground so they can build their monument and plaques. The LDS church doesn't want this. In their eyes, the church has publicly apologized and has built a monument in their honor. That's where the LDS church wants this to die. I had a meeting with the landowner and took pictures of the old crumbed rock pile that is said to be the original monument that the cavalry built. After close examination, I agreed with the landowner because the growth of the lichen and age seemed to be period to the time of the massacre. During this meeting with the landowner, historians and church officials attended the meeting.

I wasn't given a warm welcome from them. They said that they knew who I was because they saw me on TV a few days prior. During this meeting I did mention that I think we know where the original rock monument was located that the cavalry built for the victims.

They didn't pay much attention to what I had to say, which is ok. My research and investigation is my own and not everyone has to agree. Years have gone by and nothing has been settled with the land and monument dispute. I still have all my records, pictures, and even court paperwork in my protected file. This file grows every year and I will never stop my research. I still get family members from the Baker Party that reach out to me for help. I've been trying to do the right thing but I can only do so much. More people need to come out on this story. In the present day, Utah residences don't talk about the massacre and when they do, many different stories and reasoning for the murders are presented. I don't listen to these stories anymore. I go off of evidence and real history.

As you can probably imagine, the Baker Party families want closer and the story to be told. They want to visit the area without prejudice and they want to feel that they are welcomed to do so. I can stand behind this next statement and it goes with using the right history to find treasure locations.

I firmly believe that this is a legal battle that has not been resolved in over 160 years. I feel that the LDS church is controlling the history and the location by owning the land. I also think that the neighboring landowners are conflicting due to their faith in the church. I feel that the present day monument is in the wrong place and that it sits to the North East. I will strongly believe this until I find new evidence that points me in a new direction. After eleven years, my opinion and evidence has not changed.

I will stop at this point of this story. I have so much information, I am considering writing a book on the Mountain Meadows Massacre. I'm convinced that it would be a full length book about the massacre, its history, and the new evidence that I have discovered. Before I end this chapter, I would like to go back to the map that John D. Lee created. I believe it's a map to the site of where the Baker Party's belongings were buried. Before the cavalry appeared in the meadows, the people who murdered the Baker Party had time to get rid of evidence that might incriminate them. Remember how I mentioned prize horses and cattle. Those herds were not in the area once the cavalry arrived. It fact, much evidence shows that the Utah residence, involved with the murders, took the heard and spread it out in their community. These horses would have proved to be a treasure in themselves and for their community and even for profit. At one time, I was told these horses would have been worth more than any known treasure in the area.

The cattle could have fed that community for a very long time. I also mentioned the younger children that were spared. Books have been written and personal stories from the survivors have been told over the years. One interesting thing that one survivor has told about her story of being raised by a Utah family, only to notice that a few days later, her new father was riding her recently dead fathers horse. I think this story still has a lot to explain and tell. I don't know if most people can understand how deeply this story has been suppressed.

Brigham Draper (Scott Draper) Author's brother discovered old wagon parts at the site of the massacre

Here's a possible clue to the map. As a treasure hunter, I can see the partner of misdirection in it. I can see that not all things are what they seem. John D. Lee left clues to the buried treasure and its contents within the map. I know that the Baker family didn't travel all this way because they were out of money. After talking with certain, unclosed people, I've been told that a few of the wagons belonging to the Baker Party had false floors built into their wagons. Below those false floors I've been told that gold, coins, and money were stashed there so robbers could not find it. Remember the beginning of my story. I mentioned that the Arkansas people sold their properties and businesses before they ventured towards California.

Where's their belongings? Guns weren't reported found by the Cavalry when they arrived. Where did those go?

The Baker Party held the Utah people off for five days during this battle and no guns were found in the area?

I personally will let the treasure cache rest because I feel this area is a cemetery, not a pot of gold waiting to be found. If you would like to crack the case, look at the map closely. There is a section that has hidden writings that show the location of the cache. Many clues are hidden in this map. See if you can find them.

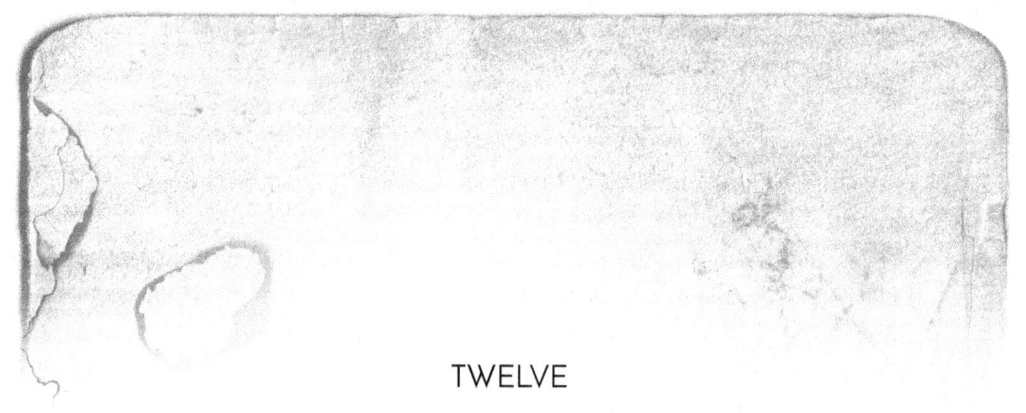

TWELVE

Lost Mines And Prospecting

Now that you know more about becoming a treasure hunter and how to find lost history, I would like to share this chapter with you. Looking for lost mines is one of my specialties and favorite things to do. Ever since I was 18 years old, I dreamed of finding and exploring lost mines. I was to visit an old ghost town and look for mines that were hidden off the beaten path, without doors and bars, so I could go inside them. For some reason mines have never made me nervous. I don't get scared of them and I can assure you, if I found one during my treasure hunts, you can count on me going inside.

For me, there's something about a mine that draws in me. I can't help myself. I have to explore it. The deeper it goes and the more passages they have, the more I enjoy it. For the record, I do like gold and silver but that's not what necessarily draws me in. It's exploring something that I know is old and forgotten by time. Standing in an old mine lets me see into the past. In a way, you can say that it's the closest I can get to seeing what it was like for an old miner from the 1800s, or a Spaniard digging for riches. During my exploring career, I have lost count of how many mines I've been in. About 5 years ago, I knew that around 150 mines were discovered and explored. I would say it safe to say that I've discovered another 20—30 since them. Now finding old mines is not easy and exploring can be more challenging due to the dangers.

I've abandoned many explorations to discover a dangerous mine. Let's go over some things to consider if you ever explore an old mine. After that, we'll get into where to look for one and some clues to make it easier to find one.

One thing I will tell you, mines are dangerous. Take it from me. I should have never just walked into my first mine I discovered. I was ready and aware of the many dangers that come from exploring a mine. The older they are, the more dangerous they become. For example, old miners, Spanish or not, would wear what is called a mine prop to hold out the ceiling. These mine props are usually trees that are cut down to an exact measurement and the prop will rest on the floor and reach to the ceiling. These mine props can be made of any type of tree species that were available in the area. Sometimes they're made of Pine trees and I've seen many made by Jupiter trees. I've been in what I called, modern mines, dating back from the early 1900s to the 1950s. In these more recently dug mines, I've discovered timers that look very similar to railroad tracks.

The older the mine, the older the mine props. If a mine is more damp, the mine props become mushy over the years and make them dangerous. Creating a mine in solid rock is the best case scenario but in all reality, most mines that I've discovered have not been solid rock mines. I've seen many mines where the ceiling has collapsed, many years before I explored it.

This is my picture above. It has timbers built around it, to stop a cave-in because the mine was dug more in the loose rock category. These can be extremely dangerous. We've all seen pictures of mine tunnels with timbers at the entrance, because many cave-ins happen at the entrance of the mine. This is because many mines were cut into unstable rock. These mines can go in for a few feet and they lead into solid rock. This means that the entrance is most likely the most dangerous spot of the mine.

I've also explored mines where the entrance was solid rock,

looking safe to me, and after walking in over a couple hundred feet, the mine becomes unstable and the solid rock turns into cracked rock, mixed in with soil. At this point, the most dangerous part of the mine is the end. This happens more often than you think. The most gut-wrecking part is when you're exploring a mine and you see a mine prop, laying on the ground, and you look up and notice loose rock on the ceiling. Sometimes it's a large boulder that appears to be hanging by a thread.

Please be careful if you come across a situation like this. It can prove to be extremely dangerous. One thing for sure, at least in my experiences, not one mine is the same or has the same dangers in it. Here's another cause for concern and this comes with older mines. Water. I don't mean water that can flood the mine, I mean water that has pooled in a puddle in the mine for hundreds of years. The pooling water itself can contain dangerous gasses, which when disturbed can release toxic gasses that can be very harmful. The best thing to do is stay away from pooling water if you enter a mine. Large amounts of water are usually a good sign. This usually means that the water is moving throughout the mine. If you find running water flowing inside the mine, this indicates that a spring or other source of water is running in and out of the mine and in most cases is safe.

Since I mentioned gasses in a mine, let's get to this other possible danger that you should be aware of. Gasses like carbon monoxide, carbon dioxide, hydrogen sulfide, and other dangerous gasses can linger in the air in the closed in space of a mine. These types of gasses are invisible and that's what makes it even more dangerous.

Let me explain.

In the 1800s, miners were very aware of gasses and how they could kill mine workers over time. They didn't have equipment and sensors like we do now these days to test the air. They relied on one simple but effective living form: a canary. It was discovered that a Canary bird was sensitive to the deadly gasses in the air of a mine. Many miners would start their day off with taking a Canary, inside a bird cage, inside the mine with them. Throughout their working day, the Canary would be a palace in the vicinity of the miners. If the Canary would react to deadly gasses, by passing out and even dying, the miners would flee the mine very quickly. This practice was used for hundreds of years and proved to be an alarm to the miners if the air was bad.

Nowadays you can buy meteors to read the oxygen levels in the mine and they will and can detect dangerous gasses in the air. These methods can help keep you out of harm's way. I would look into them if you feel you want to start exploring old mines. I'm going to explain more dangers that I've been aware of before we go more into this chapter. Your metal state and well-being. Mines is dark and cold. Some of them go very, very deep into the earth. Some mines start with one tunnel and branch off into several. Some mines are a couple hundred feet deep and some can go on for miles into the hill or mountain. You could become your worst enemy. Some people are claustrophobic and being in a mine could trigger you in a matter that you start to panic.

The walls and ceiling can feel like they are surrounding you and panic starts to come in. This is very dangerous because once you go into panic mode, your body and mind go into a fight or flight mode and then, your mind is not thinking very well. I've heard of stories where a man and his son found an old mine and entered it. They said that the mine was so large that they spent over 8 hours exploring in a day.

They explained that they found forks in the mine several times. The mine went up, down, to the right, and to the left. Their direction was gone and after a couple hours, they couldn't find the exit of where they entered. Once they realized they were lost under the ground in this mine, panic and worry started. Their panic fogged their brain and as they thought they were heading in the direction of the exit, they would go the wrong way, even deeper in the mine. Luckily the father and son finally found the way out but it took another 3 hours after they panicked. This takes a huge toll on your mind and body. Due to the hardship these two encountered, they told me that they never returned to the mine, ever and that they will never go in one again.

I will say this, I've experienced every type of danger that I have mentioned in this book. I know about panicking in a mine, I've noticed the bad air to where I couldn't get the oxygen levels I needed. I've reopened collapsed mines, only to find my nose bleeding uncontrollably within a few minutes due to the dangerous gasses in the air. I've also been lost for a short time in a mine. I was new to mine exploring and I made my mistakes but now some of them are resolved as a long term problem. Even when something bad happened to me, within a matter of a few minutes, I was out of the mine and safe. I learned from my mistakes. I learned to smell for bad gasses before I enter a mine and I only like to enter mines if I can feel a draft at the entrance.

This means that the mine has air flow from a mine vent or another entrance. I will take a can of spray paint to mark the walls of where I've been in the mine. This way I retrace my tracks once I decide to exit the mine. In my next book, I will explain more about preparing yourself before entering mines. I think this is enough information to make you aware of possible dangers. I was starting and I used common sense and it's done good for me up to date. Take your first few mine explorations slowly and carefully and you'll be fine. I know you will enjoy it and it could very much become something you like very much.

There're many different types of mines. The biggest thing about the mining process and creation of digging a mine was to follow the source of minerals. If the miner found a rich silver vein, and the vein headed in a vertical direction, that's the way the mine was dug. There's no right or wrong to digging a mine. The only wrong way is creating a mine and not following the direction of the minerals. I've been to many mines where there is a huge hole in the ground and after further expectation, I discovered the mine was over three hundred feet deep, vertically. These types of mines had a crane or elevator that lowered the workers in and out of the mine every day.

These are hard to explore unless you or someone in your team is a climber with good equipment. These vertical mine shafts can sometimes prove to be the most mysterious mines of all. The reason why is, many people can't venture into them and sometimes no one has since the miners abandoned the mine. This is where a treasure troll of wonders and possible relics can be discovered. Not to mention, you might be the first to discover it and what's inside for a hundred or even hundreds of years. Very fun and exciting stuff if you do your homework and be safe while doing it. The vertical mines, in my opinion, are some of the most dangerous. Experienced climbers will have a much easier time at it but there are even complications with that.

Many vertical mines (mine shafts) are very deep. Many shafts that I've explored are sound 30—100 feet deep and from there, many will turn into a horizontal shaft and continue on for many more hundred feet. These deep vertical shafts can be hard even for a good climber. After descending 100 feet deep and exploring it can prove to wear down the body, making it exhausting to ascend to the surface. You need to be in good shape for that. I've been in many shafts that go down 30 feet and then the shaft turns horizontally to a new level. Some of them will continue this for many different levels which makes these mines large. They can take days to explore and I don't suggest going fast.

Take your time, look for relics and tools left behind by the miners, and look for virgin minerals as well. Finding relics and/or tools can help you learn who the original miners were. It can also help you know what time period the mine was created. By finding objects left behind by others, you can carbon test many things. Wood, metals, paper, leather, and many other things can be tested by carbon testing. This is a great way to get dates on relics. If you don't want to do that, then another way to get a date is reaching out to others on social media that have spent many years in the field. I know many people that have been metal detecting for years that know a lot. Other known treasure hunters can get a good idea as well.

Knowing the date of a mine, objects, and structures is very important! This is how you can tell if you found something from the mining, Spanish, outlaw, era. These types of discoveries can be common if you find a mine that has not been discovered by someone before you. This is where the name "Lost Mine" comes from. If the mine is lost, then the location has been unclear to hunters and prospectors. You can prove or disprove that with being one of the lucky people to stumble across a lost mine. Vertical mines are more common than it may seem. Sometimes miners would create a vertical shaft purely for a ventilation shaft, connected at a different end of the mine to create air flow, good air circulation. This is important because if a mine is very deep in the ground or in the mountain, air can get very thin in the mine so miners created an air shaft.

Sometimes the vertical shaft is for the entrance and/or exit. Sometimes they were created to lift ore and minerals out of the ground. There's many reasons why vertical shafts are used in mining, back in the day and in modern times.

Now let's talk about horizontal mines and tunnels. I want to make sure we cover these different types of mines so you may have a chance of spotting them while you're out in the field. Looking for a horizontal mine is in many ways the same as looking for a vertical shaft. I like to refer to the horizontal mine as a tunnel shaft or tunnel. These are the same traditions that you see on TV during shows or even in Hollywood. These are my favorite kinds because they're fairly easy or easier to enter than a shaft. I've spent a lot of time in mine tunnels and I can cover ground, rather than worrying about the climbing gear and more, just to enter the tunnel. I can usually just go right in after I discover and inspect the safety of the tunnel's entrance.

Mine Shaft Opening about 12 feet from ground level—
Found by Author

The mine tunnel entrance shown in the above photo is an exception because of the unsafe level of the tunnel itself. The entrance is about 12 feet or so. I was not able to enter it and explore. In this case, I would tell you to bring a ladder but I can't see one of us, caring around 20 feet later, through the wilderness, on foot for situations like this. It's not practical. I'll have to leave it for another time. This mine was found on the Utah-Nevada state border.

Another to keep in mind is that just because it starts as a safe looking tunnel entrance, it doesn't mean

From there everything is good. I have been in many tunnels that were safe, no bad gasses, no threat of the ceiling caving in. No major dangers except one, a deep hole in the ground. This is where another matter comes into play. You need a good flashlight, nice and bright.

I've inspected these types of combination mines that start off horizontal and with many of a few feet inside, to a thousand feet inside, a vertical shaft was dug, right in the middle of the walkway. Like I said early in this chapter, you have to follow the minerals. I want you to consider this as well, you will find many mines in your days of searching where the state park, National Park, Forest Service, or the BLM has covered the mine entrance with bricks, iron bars, and sometimes with dirt. This is due to safety. Because of situations like people getting lost, falling in holes, and so on, they get covered up. I believe it's because people exploring weren't prepared for the dangers.

That's why I keep bringing up situations. I don't want to send you outdoors with the knowledge of what to look for without telling and warning you about hazards too.

Now let's begin on how to find these lost mines. You can find mines easily by researching old mines back in the 1880s from your area. Many states have not updated the laws of stating a claim since 1872. If minerals have been found and a miner and/or prospector wants to work it, they have to follow the laws and claim that area for themselves. Stating a claim is fairly easy. You go down to your local county office, state office and ask for the proper paperwork to file a claim. It requires you to fill in your name, the location of the minerals found, and what minerals you are mining. Easy stuff. It's been like this since 1872. I've spent a lot of time in my local county office, going through old paperwork of mining claim paperwork in my area. I've found many lost mines by doing this step. Some states have digitized these records and now you can go online and find old mining information from your computer or phone.

I want to add another step that the miner, current time or past times, had to literally state the property lines of a claim. Now, this may differ from state to state a little but you'll get the idea. The reason why it's called "Stating a Claim" is because you have to mark the four corners of your mine. Some states require a rock cairn built at the four corners and some allow wood posts to be placed. The laws say that the posts or rock piles need to be tall. Most states require 3 to 4-foot-tall, in fact. So now, you can find records, locations, names, minerals present and, you can find the old states. It sounds too easy but it can prove to be a little harder than you think. This type of information will get you close to the vicinity. Your eyes will have to do the rest of the work.

I did mention mining laws of 1872, that means many mines before that year were not stated. You also have to consider that there's mention that many people illegally mined and is still happening today. That means you will not find the records of course. If you're looking for Spanish mines and even older mines, you will have to go back to a Spanish Waybill or map to locate it with records. Finding old records like I suggested will get you in the right area. Try that and see what you find. There's more. The United States recognizes two different types of mines. There's a lode mine and a placer mine.

The load mine is your traditional mine with the horizontal and/or vertical entrance and the placer mine is an open pit mine. Open pit mines are more common in modern days. A lode mine allows a person to claim a stretch of 1,500 feet long and 600 feet wide for one claim. A placer mine allows a person to claim a 5, 10, 40, and even up to 160 acres per mine claim. If you're looking for state posts, keep that in mine. The mine is usually, somewhat centered within those boundaries. Not always though so keep that in mind as well. I suggest you do your homework on starting a mining claim in your area. See if the laws have changed in the last 150 years. This way you know what to look for. This can help in locating old mines.

I'm going to let you in on a trade secret that I've learned throughout the years. This may help you if you're having trouble finding a mine in a certain area.

I was looking for an old Spanish mine, around twelve years ago. I found many clues like structures, Spanish symbols on rocks and trees, and rock monuments in the area. I searched for another 3 years, still with no luck finding the old mine. I looked up and down the mountain. I looked in every canyon nearby. I knew I was close because I found the Spanish smelter but I couldn't find mine. I was stuck! I sat on the site for a while and pushed it aside. About 2 years later, I remembered seeing some dry creek beds and running creeks in the area. Suddenly I had an idea. I thought back and remembered that some of these nearby creeks had shiny minerals that I could see with the right sun shine. I passed these creeks for years and didn't pay much attention to the minerals.

I guess I wasn't surprised because the Spanish obviously mined there for those minerals. Then I came up with an idea. I decided to go back out in the field and start collecting samples of the soils. I set in many test samples to see if gold or silver was present in the area. These test samples also include the value of the minerals. The assay would show me not only what minerals were in the area but also how much. I know that Spanish went for rich silver and gold so I decided to run many tests and sent them to an assayer. On each sample tube, I mark the area with a 1-12. Then I marked the numbers on a topographic map so I know where I test number 1 and/or number 7 and so on. At the time, each assay cost me around $100 dollars. It was a little bit of an investment but I think it was worth it.

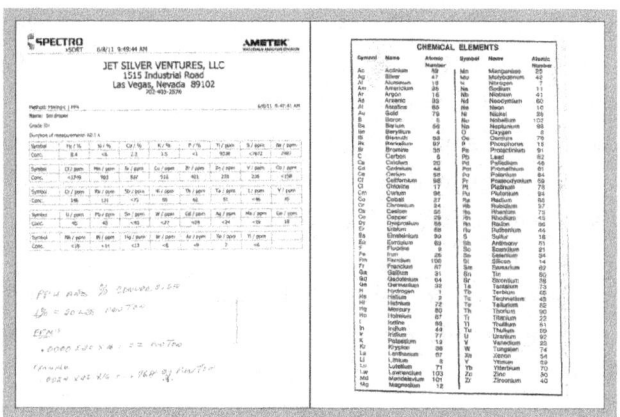

One of the twelve Mining Assays from the Area of Minerals and Old Spanish Mine

I found that one of my assay tests did reveal silver and titanium. This is exactly what I was looking for. I noticed that it was from the assay tube labeled # 6. I had it marked on my topographic map (use a 7.5-minute topographic map) and I had the area. It took some time but later that year, I found the old Spanish silver mine I was looking for. I discarded those other assays because they didn't contain silver or gold. The old Spanish silver mine I founded was only up the dry creek and around the corner from where I took the assay. It had a very small entrance, looked almost like a cave hole about 4 feet in diameter. The entrance had a lot of vegetation and dirt pilling around it. I most likely would have missed it if it wasn't for assaying the area.

This is where I learned to prospect as you're tracking a lost mine. I have many assays and I keep them in my files that are attached to the area, legends, and clues that I have recovered. I suggest you do the same. Keep record of your discoveries. Where, when, and what is very important. Treasure hunting is an investment into your hobby or career. Keep your records up to date and separated from other stories and locations. Do not share your discoveries with anyone unless you tend to not keep it safe anymore. I only trust a few people.

Family and friends are always saying to me, "I know you don't want to tell me." Prospecting is a great tool to learn and use in the field. If you want to be a treasure hunter, you need to learn many ticks of the trade. Think of it as you wear many hats. Sometimes you're an investigator. Sometimes you're the grunt labor.

I want to share some more information with you about looking for mines. I think this will help a lot in the field.

What's the one thing that you will always have when you dig a hole? Dirt and rock.

No one can start to carve their way into a hill or mountain without creating earthly rubble. The same goes with mining. Miners always have to discard all the rock and dirt that they remove from the earth. It has to go somewhere. In the era of the great mining times, like the Gold Rush, miners weren't too worried about leaving their mine dump. Most of the time they would discard their trash a few feet out from the entrance. This would create a pile of dirt and rock, compiling down below the mine entrance. If the mine was on a slope, it would start to create piles, full of different colors of rubble that can be seen from a distance. Some of these mine dumps are small. Sometimes the mine dumps are extremely large and you can see them from miles away.

If the mine was dug in a few hundred feet, you can figure to find a dump about the size of a small house. If the mine was deeper than that, you can find that these dumps can be the size of a football field. This makes it easier for you. Keep your eyes out for disturbed dirt and rock piles. Look in the close proximity for a mine entrance. Now if it was a vertical mine shaft, it was more common to see several piles of dirt around the mine entrance. Small piles could be as large as a truck and some or smaller than that. These older mines were dug by hands and tools, not heavy equipment like in today's day.

I'm going to let you in on another trade secret.

Miners that illegally mined would sometimes spread their mine dump throughout the vicinity. Blend it in with mother nature so someone else could not find the waste dumping very easily. If the mine was owned by a one-man crew, he might have done the same thing. This keeps your mine secret and it happened more than you think. Let's go back even further in time. The Spanish were great miners and had thousands of years of experience passed down for generations. They were tricky and knew that if they found a rich mine, their mine dump would grow far too large to keep its location secret from others. Because many Spanish mining parties had slaved labor, they would have a group of slaves do nothing else, all day, every day but spreading mine dump all around the vicinity.

They didn't want their mines to be found. This is also why the Spanish, for many situations, created a small entrance to the mines. It was easier to cover up the hole and then return to rework it at a later date. This is why Spanish clues and symbols are marked on trees and rocks. So they or another group of Spaniards could return after the winter or long journey from Mexico and find the hidden mine. I'm telling you, the Spanish were good at what they did. It would pay off for you to learn as much as you can about the Spanish mining process. The same goes for miners in the 1800s. If it was a large legal mining company, other security was set in place to protect their mine and investments. If it was a small mining group, they tended to be much more secret. Look below to see a Spanish mine entrance.

Author kneeling at Old Spanish Mine Entrance

This Spanish mine entrance is not much bigger than mine. When I entered it, I had to lay down on my back and shimmy into it. Once I was inside, the ceiling to the mine was large enough to stand up. The walls of the mine were around six to 8 feet wide. The mine appears to be small but the mine inside is much larger. It was hidden by vegetation in the area. We call these types of mine entrances called a "Coyote Hole." This is because it looks like a coyote hole or a wolf den. It's just small enough to cover it and conceal it with a large rock, vegetation, mud and sticks, anything the Spanish could use to keep the entrance hidden. This is somewhat of a common way the Spanish made their mines.

It does depend on the group of Spaniards that created it. You can't just look at a mine and know who did it. It takes some investigation and sometimes, more than others. Spanish mines are the same as 1800s mines when it comes to tunnels and direction. I've been in Spanish mines that go up and down small angled slopes. I've seen them turn to the right, the left. I've seen some that I call Swiss cheese. If I was to draw a side view of the mine, it would look like a slice of Swiss cheese. One thing that you can look for is tool marks on the ceiling and walls. Newer mines can show signs of electrical hammers while the ancient mines were dug by chisels and hammers.

Another thing to keep in mind, old prospectors were no dummies. If an old prospector came across an old mine, worked many years before him, and noticed that it still had minerals and a good chance of striking it rich, he would rework it in a more modern way. This has confused mine explorers in the past because they appear more modern. I've researched old Spanish mines and I've been taken to the site by others and shown a mine that looks to me like it was made in the late 1800s. Later I would hear that old timers have past the legend around that they found old iron tools and found items that sound like they came from Spanish slave workers.

After checking into the local legend I learned that many people believe that the miner from the 1800s, when reworked, made the entrance bigger so it was easier to carry ore and dumps out of the mine. I heard that he continued on in the mine and carved the walls again with modern day tools and got what the Spanish didn't. Some told me that if I went deeper in the mine I'm speaking of, I would see a mixture of tools marks from the Spanish in the late 1600s and tools marks from the miner in the 1800s. I have not been able to prove this 100% but I will tell you that it's a very good possibility.

I've researched many stories like that. I've read journals and documents that state a person found an old abandoned mine with strange ancient tools found inside. Only to find that same mine and it looks like a modern mine, large in size. I've seen evidence of large mining companies that arrived in an area, and blasted the old mine to mine in their methods. I want to be aware of this so you can learn that not all things are as they appear. Listen to the old timers' stories. Read your history and investigate. Nothing is impossible. Nothing is set in stone. You're that investigator, the scientist, and the storyteller once you have enough experience and knowledge. Let the clues tell you where to go next. If you see something that doesn't look natural, most likely it's not.

I'm going to share another picture of mine with you. This is a typical mine that you will find in and around an old ghost town, also known as a mining town or camp. I think it will help you see the differences between mine. Don't read a mine by its cover. Make sure you learn as much as you can about mines if you want to be an expert.

What a Typical Mine from the 1800s Looks Like

Speaking of ghost towns and mining camps. If you happen to live in a place that has an old ghost town, known for mining in your area, explore it. This will help you notice mines, dumps and entrances. This is how I learned and started out. When I was 18 years old, I explored as many old mining towns as I could in Arizona, Idaho, Utah, and other surrounding states. I visited them often and spent many years doing so. I've seen so many mines, I learned what to look for. I'm going to tell you I know the smell of mines now too. It sounds weird but I have spent so much time in mines, I know what they smell like and as I'm looking for a mine, I can usually smell it if I'm within a couple hundred feet from it.

You never forget the smell and your noise can help guide you if you and your brain makes a mental note of the smell. I would like to talk more about mines but you still have more to learn if you want to be an explorer. I'll go more into details about mines in another book. Take care if you take on the life of exploring mines. Take my experiences with you and stay out of danger. Refer back to this chapter if you need to be reminded of dangers and hazards. No mine is worth mining for. I'll give you one more thing to remember and consider. Mines will always stay put. They're not going anywhere. Keep a GPS system with you.

There's many apps for phones to mark it on a map. Regroup if you need to think about the task in front of you. As long as you have the location marked, Longitude and latitude, you can go home for years, come back and revisit the mine. Once you practice this way of being patient and careful, you'll learn that you have all the time in the world to explore smart and safely.

THIRTEEN

Exploring Ghost Towns And Their Treasures

Really like exploring ghost towns and some states have many more to see than others, that's for sure. If I come up missing for days, check the closest mother of ghost towns near me because I just enjoy visiting them. To stand on the boardwalk of a saloon is very exciting. Just think of all the people that walked down that same boardwalk over 100 years ago.

Can you imagine the gunfights that took place?

Ghost towns are truly a huge part of America history but even going deeper than that, there were the true dreams and hopes of our county. During the Gold Rush era, everyone and their dog left their homes in hopes that they could strike it rich. Men left their families, hoping to send for them later and even though this happened, it was also common for the man not to return home or ever be seen again. Boom towns (ghost towns) like Tombstone had more to offer than just gold and silver. Doc Holiday and Wyatt Earp make history from this town. It wasn't just them that left their mark there. The outlaws did their fair share of trouble in Tombstone.

You can still visit Tombstone today and take a trip back in time and see what it was like in the 1800s. It's pretty eye opening stuff. To walk into the Bird Cage Theater is almost overwhelming. You can still see bullet holes in the ceilings of this building. The OK Corral is still there as well. Can you just picture what the town thought when that gun fight took place? Arizona has tons of historical places to see along with Nevada and many more. If you want western, you have to go see it. Now you just don't have to see old western towns to find a ghost town. There's more modern day ghost towns around the world.

Take Hashima Island in Japan for an example. This place was booming in the 1950s. It was a place for workers and their families to call home. By the 1970s, this area that housed thousands was deemed unlivable and people moved out of the area. Today, the old ruins of apartment type living can still be seen. Here's another example, Pripyat Ukraine is possibly a place that you've heard of. You may know it as Chernobyl. The town that housed over 49,000 workers and their families had to abandon the area and town due to the realtor meltdown at the nuclear plant. Today, the area is still radioactive and the ruins are decaying away. This wasn't that long ago either. We're talking about the year 1986.

Here's another interesting modern ghost town that is abandoned today: Centralia, Pennsylvania. This was a mining town of a population of over 2,761 residents who lived at this location in 1980. Due to an accidental fire in the coal mine itself, the town slowly started to lose the battle. The mine was shut down, and after several years, the town died, too. The burning coal fire is still active today. Experts say that it will burn for many more years. Some people go to visit this town to see the homes still standing. There's still some mines operating in the area but this town is dead. Breathing air in the area is full of fumes. Now, I would like to ask you, what is a ghost town after hearing this information? It's a place where people once lived but now it's nothing but dead.

Exploring old buildings is very popular as well. There Are thousands of old warehouses, malls, fairgrounds, mansions, and so much more abandoned, not only in the United States but around the world. Have you heard of the Randall Park Mall in Cleveland, Ohio? This mall is a great example of who things were not too long ago and how things die. This mall was built in 1976 as a large mall that thrived until the last few years before it closed in 2009. Photographs have been taken and it's quite a thing to see. Many warehouses around the world are still standing but no one is there. Silence had overcome these sites. I'm willing to bet, no matter where you live, you can find an abandoned place that once was alive.

Now let's talk about ghost towns from the 1800s. This picture below was a ranch house that soon became a tavern in the west along the Old Spanish Trail.

This old home was built in the mid 1800's and served its purpose for sure. It's still standing today. Could you imagine finding this and exploring it? This is an example of what I'm talking about. Let's take a look at something that is just as old but has a completely different feel to it. The old wood type buildings from booming towns in the 1800s.

Dodge City Gunsmoke Movie Set

Even though the picture above is a movie set prop from the Gunsmoke show, it shows you what these types of buildings look like today. In the west, there are still many places you can visit today that look like this. Unfortunately, they all disappear with time. That's why I'm going to continue this chapter with old fashioned ghost towns of the old west.

It's true, soon many of our children will not be able to read about the old days and then go out to see what's left for themselves. I've been visiting many ghost towns now for over 20 years and I've seen great old structures that are standing one year, then a couple years later, they're gone. Old history like this is disappearing and sometimes it's from new development of modern day cities, sometimes it's people destroying them, and sometimes it's father time and mother nature. Exploring ghost towns is what really got me going on researching as much as I about history. It's an eye opener for me to see what has come and gone in my life of exploring and researching. I can only imagine what it's like for my parents and grandparents. The bottom line is I believe these sites of old structures are a treasure but there's more. Treasure has always followed where people lived and worked. If an old timer had a claim up in the mountains, chances are he buried a little cache outside of his mining shack. Most of the time they would bury it just outside the window of the shack.

That way they can sit in their chair and watch for anyone who may come and try to take it. I can tell you that this is something that happens, possibly more often than you think. If you would like to look more into this, I suggest reaching out to a good metal detector. Someone that has been shining a detector for a while. Those guys know how to anticipate possible finds. They spent many years hunting for relics and they've been in many situations that help them find treasure that have been left behind.

Because of these booming towns, many people can for pleasure, to strike it rich, business ventures, women, and so much more. Just think of the possibilities that could have been left behind. Here's an example, fires. Many mining towns were abandoned due to a fire that broke out and burnt down the whole area. Sometimes they rebuilt, if the gold, silver, and business were thriving, but many times people moved on. We're talking about many valuables and even bored little caches in the area that were never retrieved. I want to show you an example of what I'm talking about. This way you can understand that lost treasures and history can be found. Not just littles treasures either.

Let's take the town of Bodie, California. In the 1880s, Bodie was a huge town prospering from its mines and businesses. Bodie was a big booming town when it came to gold. It's said that over $38 million dollars of gold and silver was spent from 1877 to the end of the late 1800s. Bodie didn't stop there. In its prime, Bodie had 10,000 residents that once lived there during the booming times. Many residents stayed and lived in Bodie long after the price of gold and silver dropped. In fact, the town wasn't really abandoned until the 1940s. We're talking about a huge town with many buildings, mills, stores, and homes. If you do some research, you find hundreds of great pictures that show that town the way it is today. These buildings that I speak of, many of them are still standing. There are more, a lot more.

I don't have to explain to you what happened in the booming mining industry today in the old days. You can imagine the kind of money spent there for hotels, gambling, women, and more. If you were a person looking for fun, money, gold, you name it, Bodie was the palace to go to in the western states. You also should understand that this town wasn't only a party place and a money making machine, Bodie has residents who had families, they went to church, and kids went to school. It would have been a site to see back in the old days. A fire broke out in 1892 and a lot of the town was destroyed on the west side of Main Street. The town rebuilt their buildings and life moved on, Bodie was reborn. Another fire took place by a boy playing with matches in 1932. Unfortunately, it destroyed some of the town too. At this point, not many residents lived in the town, which was the start of decaying and death for Bodie.

The prices of gold and silver dropped and it was almost impossible for the mining companies to make a profit. So again, the town continued to die. Some residents remained in Bodie, even until the time of their death. Some history explains that the harsh summer heat played a role in Bodies decrease during the 1930 - 1940s. Even though the town still had many buildings, the town and its residence were forgotten. By 1961, the State of California made Bodie a National Historical Park. What the park preserved is still, in my eyes, one of the best things any state could have done. Instead of rebuilding it, they preserved and protected the town and its belongings.

What I'm about to tell you, may blow your mind. It's hard to comprehend this type of thing in the modern world. The reason it was so obvious to protect the historical town is because the town appeared to be untouched my man when the state started to go to work on the park. Over 100 buildings were still standing and in decent shape. Cars were still parked in the front of homes. House still had furniture like chairs, couches, and even beds with blankets and pillows. Dining tables had cups and silverware on them, like someone was there just early that day. The general store shelves were stocked with goods. The bars and gambling halls had poker chips like Vegas is today.

 Churches had the Holy Bible sitting on the pews. It was like standing there in time of what Body looked like back in the 1800s, only without people. This town stood in time as a masterpiece. You could look at pictures from the internet, it will make you really take you back in time. This great place is still under watch by the Park Rangers every day. Thousands of people visit it every year. You can still see the buildings and belongings that I spoke of from a small distance away. Unfortunately, I have not taken any pictures to show you at this point. Surf the internet and you'll see what I mean.

Places like this are not only a once in a lifetime opportunity. I, myself have found my own little piece of abandoned town in the desert. In 2016, My wife LeeAnn and I went on an adventure drive down an old paved road that we've never been on before. We were on a small vacation, looking for coyotes to hunt. The day prior, we spent the day riding 4-wheelers on the east boundaries of town. The next day, we decided to drive south out of town. This has always been our thing. LeeAnn and I have made many great discoveries by just picking a road and driving down it.

If we haven't explored a mountain range or old road, leading to who knows where, we have to go and see it. After about 20 minutes

Treasures of the Ancients 133

of driving out of town, we found ourselves in a very secluded area, no homes, no town. As far as we could see, we saw nothing but rolling hills and nothing but desert. We approached a bend in the road with an old bridge and a river running under it. Then we both saw old buildings ahead. As we approached the area very slowly, we saw what looked like old abandoned buildings.

We pulled the car over and discovered that we were right. A weird feeling overcomes us and we're feeling confused about what we were looking at and why this palace was just abandoned on an old road. What we discovered next was even more overwhelming.

We exited our vehicle and started walking towards the buildings as we noticed that a lot of belongings were on the ground, in vegetation, and spread all around the site. The area was becoming more full of dirty and old things like dolls, furniture, blankets, clothes, trash, and more. I took a step back, pondering on what we were going to see.

Are there homeless people here? What happened to this place?

I couldn't decide if we just made a great discovery or if we witnessed a war zone. It was truly creepy and at the same time, fascinating. I noticed that LeeAnn was about 50 feet in front of me, just exploring and I decided to run up beside her so we could stay together. My guard was high at this point. Oh my gosh, what we saw next still intrigues me.

Each and every building was full of belonging like the people who lived there just up and lifted their homes in a hurry. Like if they were there one minute and then the next, they were gone. Sure time and weather destroyed the place and decade the belongings left behind but it was strange.

Many of the buildings were just in a mess. Dressers, beds, tables, refrigerators, and some much more were found in their resting place. Again, I looked around like I was in a horror movie. Curiosity was still in LeeAnn's soul as she kept moving forward to another building and another building. I remained near her just in case. After about 20 minutes, I realized that there has not been a hint of people around. No homeless people, and no one driving down the old road to this place. I was able to drop my guard and that's when the explorer in me took over. I started taking pictures and paying attention to the age of the belonging.

We found canned food, stoves, and more. The area looked like a bomb exploded in this area and stuff was everywhere. After a while, we were relieved that it seemed that it's been abandoned for a few years now. The building reminded me of something that was built in a cheap manner about 30 years prior to us visiting this site. We left everything behind and undisturbed. We did take a lot of pictures though. I'll leave more below so you can see what we saw in our eyes.

LeeAnn and I left the area after an hour or so of exploring and taking pics but this place is still in my mind. I know that there are many other places like this in North America. Because of our discovery, I went home and still today, I read and learn about more places like this.

I discovered that there are many around the world. If you think that you can't find something like this, think again. I know you can. Let's move back to ghost towns of the past and the possible treasures that could be waiting to be found. There's nothing to think of when it comes to treasures in and around an old ghost town, people coming and going. Everything from daily mail to a stagecoach full of supplies entered and exited a booming town, sometimes every day. Now, think of the outlaws sitting back in those days, just looking for something of value to steal.

Do you know how many stagecoaches were robbed from the 1800s to the 1900s?

Neither do I, but when you get to the back of this book, I have treasure sites, locations, people names, and the value of treasures still lost today. Around 20% of these treasures that I mention are from outlaws robbing and stealing. That's a lot. This type of thing happened every day in the old days of the wild west. When I say wild west, I don't mean just Arizona, California, and Nevada—I mean the United States as a whole. Not to mention how many people that traveled down the Oregon Trail with their families and valuable items. Many people were killed by natives and that's where their belongings are still today, in the ground.

Outlaws would steal gold and silver from a prospector in the mountains, only to be chased by a posse. When this happened, the outlaws buried their treasure and many of them were caught and hanged, never to return to claim their prize. The possibilities of treasures are endless. You just have to know where to look. Knowing the legends of your area will help you. Let's take into consideration that famous known outlaws like Butch Cassidy, Jesse James, and Billy the Kid, and so many more. Did they only live in the mountains? Absolutely not. In fact, many outlaws are reported coming in and out every day. Day after day. Time after time. Moving on from one town to another. These famous outlaws came with a group of outlaws as well. Some of these outlaw groups stayed together until the end of their lives. Many spread up or moved onto their own lives in other places.

This is how I know that outlaw and bandit treasures are all over the United States. I'm not the only person in the U.S. that knows these legends. Many people are out on the weekend, looking for their next discovery. I want to give you the stories and information so you can go out and find some too. Make your mark in history, by finding lost history. You need to bring your own investigator and go out there and find these treasures. All you need is the drive, some information, and the right tools, including a little luck, to find your treasure.

FOURTEEN

Get To Know Your Local History

This section of this book is going to help you know what to research and how to get information about legends and treasures in your area. I'm going to explain what I have done. By doing this, I hope it helps you in your area. When I moved to Boise Idaho, I knew nothing about the area. Idaho is a beautiful place with a lot of offices. Living in Boise itself, it didn't feel like it had much history and adventures to offer. My impression of the area was, if you like a decent sized city, it's not a bad place. By the time I was 19 years old, I found something new about the area, a large ski resort.

    I traveled up the mountain to the ski lift several times and it was really pretty, winter, fall, spring, or summer but I didn't see much but a normal mountain with pine trees. After a few trips to the top of that mountain, I stopped on the side of the road. The scenic view displayed the city itself but I was able to see a lot further than just the city. I could see the hills to the south. I was able to look to the east and west. I saw more mountains and high desert landscapes. That's when I realized at that time, there must be more than I know. For the next few months, I started learning as much as I could about the area and its history. I visited the old penitentiary museum at the eastside of town.

This is when I decided, I needed to spread out my search and see what else was in the area. My dad and I took a road trip about an hour east of Boise to a town named Idaho City. This is where I knew, I was finding more things that I like. Idaho City is a place that people can still visit today, to see the historic tourist attraction of the old mining days. Here you can take your family and walk the main street and visit the old buildings of Idaho City. Most of the buildings are a business or small museum. One of the buildings we visited had a place with a gold pan and workers to help you learn how to do it on your own.

I was hooked. I still remember Idaho City very well. We drove to the north of the town a few miles and saw the old mines and mine dumps of the 1800s. We pretty much spent the whole day there and I learned all I could about the history in the area. It was a good place to do so. I asked a question to one of the museum employees, "Is Idaho City the oldest mining town in the area?" She replied by showing me a map of Idaho and she was nice enough to show me other places that had mining towns in southeastern Idaho. She pointed to McCall Idaho and Silver City Idaho. I visited McCall a few times and made my fair share of gold panning the river that was along the highway.

From visiting McCall, I once again spread out my search. My brother David lived in Idaho as well a couple years later. I started to tell him about all the places I learned about. I lived in the area for a couple years at that point. I was recently married to LeeAnn at this point and LeeAnn and I decided to take a road trip to the southwest border of Idaho and Nevada. Guess what we did during this trip? You may have got it right. There was a side dirt road that traveled for around 100 miles that in my mind was a short cut. It wasn't much of a short cut but it was worth it. After about one and half hours into our trip, we ended up at a great site called Silver City Idaho. This is a famous old mining town that some say is the queen of all ghost towns.

Some local residents in Silver City bought and restored the old hotel, church, and a few more buildings on the main street. They did a great job and it was like going back in time. The saloon is restored well and the main street still has the old boardwalk, connecting the downtown buildings together. LeeAnn spent only a small amount of time there that day but I figured I would be back. David, my brother, decided he wanted to go back with me the next year during spring. The snow and winters can get bad up there in those mountains and I waited patiently for the snow to melt. I had a 4x4 at the time which proved to be in my favor.

David and I spent a whole day in town, talking to the store and hotel owners. They like old mining history as much as I did. Even more because they bought the land and buildings to preserve the town. The man that owned the hotel at the time had a lot and I mean a lot of information and history about Silver City. It sent me on my way for the next couple years. David and I revisited the old town the next year but instead of exploring downtown, we explored the outer boundaries. The hotel owner sold me a topographic map the year prior that showed me all the mines that rested there. I had the exact location and names of the mines.

David and I took old dirt roads that sometimes looked like a wagon trail. This is why I'm glad I had a 4x4 vehicle. We must have explored over 20 mines. We found all kinds of relics and old structures. We explored many mines too. I learned a lot about the area but I also learned a lot about mines. Silver City was a perfect training ground for me. Many years later, I moved to St. George, Utah, in 2010. LeeAnn and I were attending Dixie University. This is where I was studying history and anthropology. I knew nothing about the local history once again. I had to find a new training ground. This area wasn't as blessed with old ghost towns like the Boise Idaho area was but I did find a place called Silver Reef.

Silver Reef was a great place to visit and now, I've been there over 50 times to explore or more. These mines and some old structures at this location. After about a year, I wanted more. I needed to find and explore more so I started inquiring around, just like the other places I lived before. By 2011, I had many leads on old Spanish stories, pioneer legends, and more. This is around the time I got involved with the Mountain Meadows Massacre site. I learned that the Spanish came into the area in the late 1700s. I was on a mission.

To research and discover as much as I could. When I was finished with school, I returned back to full-time work but that didn't stop me from learning more.

My oldest brother Scott came to live in St. George for a couple of years and we found a lot together. I learned by having someone with me that likes the same kind of things, really helped my search. Luckily I have two brothers that I was able to go on many adventures with. Still today when I talk to them on the phone, we revisit our memories of our explorations. How can this be a bad thing? It's not. Treasure hunting and historical research has only brought me closer to people. How about a treasure? It's all how you look at things.

I became friends with people in the area that helped point me in the right direction to lost history. I explored every weekend that I could in the desert. In the high mountains that surrounded St. George. I learned and studied all that I could. Before I knew it, people started to know me as the treasure hunter and historical researcher. Locals would tell me their stories and show me locations where they found interesting stuff. I was a reporter and investigator by this time. Not for a newspaper but for myself and the people in the area that enjoyed history and a good adventure. Word started to travel from my experiences and knowledge of the area and before I knew it, I had more locations and legends to investigate than I could handle.

I started to get phone calls to be on a newspaper article and things snowballed from that point on. I was surprised at the time how many people were like me. People were sharing a lot about their adventures with me and I did the same back. I can't even tell you how many meetings I've had with people in St. George at a restaurant, talking about treasures and history. All of this happened because of my persistence and passion to lose history. I've always been good at talking with people and getting to know them. I like to share stories and other people do too. I learned by being real with them, they did the same to me.

I wasn't out to do anything but find history and explore. A treasure here and there was enough for me. I learned that the treasure was in the knowledge and the relationships I was making. I still live in St. George today. I don't know if I could ever leave after all this work I've done. In my spare time, I learned about other places and treasures. Now, I have a team of treasure hunters and investigators and we go out as much as we can. Exploring and investigating new sites.

I can't tell you how many hours I've spent on researching. I stopped counting after several thousands of hours looking into the past. Now, I can help others. I can point people in the right direction, and I can help mentor them to their riches, whatever that might be. I worked my butt off and it paid off. I'm doing what I like to do and I couldn't see myself doing anything else. You can do the same thing. You have to want it. You have to work hard at it, and you really have to love what you do. If you have the passion and drive, everything will fall into place, if you're patient. Time will be on your side but you have to earn it. You can't expect to find the motherlode in a week, not a month, or even a year. You have to really want it.

I told you this life story of mine in a nut shell because I was just a young man, wanting to learn. I'm in my 40's now and I still go out and learn more. I find and hear about new places all the time. People email often with new discoveries. I want to help you do the same thing if that's what you choose. If you are not meant to do this type of thing, reaching out to people and exploring the outdoors, that's okay too. I have never had a person look at me after telling one of my stories and then say "I hate that" or "That's boring". It's because it's not. I can point people in the right direction and mentor them or I can entertain them with a good story. Either way, it's a win, win.

If you want to do something like I explained above, do the same thing. Get to know your area and the people in the area. I have found that the credibility is great when a person tells me that they are the son of so and so, who found this at this place. They started saying, my father told me about so and so and I went with him at the time he found this.

See how that works. A person who says and/or heard a legend from a family member?

These types of people and stories have proved to be good for me.

I've never been pointed in the wrong direction for a person who has first-hand experience or story. Usually, not even a second-hand or third-hand experience from a family member. You will never know what is in store for you until you try. Give it time and learn more about your area. Ask questions when you find someone that wants to share stories with you. Give back to the community and help find lost history and treasures. This is the way it works everywhere in the world. Did you know that in Europe, more than 70% of the new discoveries, treasure, relics, and lost history are found by a scholar or explorer?

Same goes with archeology and anthropology. Most of the times when you see a new discovery made in the world, whether it's a lost city in the jungle or an underground tunnel system, is it from a local person? Families that have lived in an area for generations, have a lot of information. The tricky part is getting them to trust you. That way, you will know how to learn on your own. I have many sites that I will never talk about or point someone to. That's something that my mentor and parents taught me. When you say you're going to do something, you better do it.

When you shake hands with a person that just shared information with you and they mention that you can never tell, don't ever tell anyone. Word does travel in the treasure hunting community. If you get a target on your back as a dishonest person, that will stay with you forever. If you break your promise, they will never trust you again. Your name and credibility will be lost, just like many treasures I'm looking for. Stay true to your word and never give a person or group the reason to say that you can't be trusted. I hope this helps you. Like I said, if you're looking to be entertained, I have stories. If you're looking to learn, take it from me. After 26 years of being a treasure hunter, I've learned a lot of lessons.

I want to leave you with a thought. Treasure hunters have been known to be bad people in our society today. For many generations, people have said that treasure hunters are out for their own personal gain. I've met many, many treasure hunters, big or small, and I can tell you that only about 1% of these hunters have been bad people or selfish hunters. Most of them like to hear and tell their stories. Most of us try to uncover mysteries and lost history. I have heard this many times before, out of the other months, "If I find a treasure, that's just a bonus".

Do these people sound back to you?

I hate to say it but in my time, I think that only untrustworthy people I've met with and spoken to, are the officials that control our history. Laws and regulations are pitiful in some states. I've known people that have found treasures and made new discoveries and all they wanted was credit. These ones that I speak of have made deals with their states officials and given up their rights to the treasure. Only to ask that the artifacts, documents, or riches are put in a museum with their name on it. Some of them have asked for a finder's fee. These stories that I have been involved with have never turned out to be good for the hunter.

Nothing that was promised happened. I ask you, who's the historical thief? Who's suppressing history and new discoveries? I think after reading this far in my book, you know what I think and you know who I'm talking about. You decide for yourself. Start reaching and getting out there on your own adventure and path to treasures. Not all treasures are shiny. Not all of them are what you see in Hollywood. Sometimes a treasure can be a new friendship. Someone you can share your experiences with. Sometimes it is a lost ghost town in your area. Sometimes it may be a cave full of artifacts. You decide that on your own.

Author holding a Spanish Sword

What is a treasure? It's what you make of it.

FIFTEEN

Start Exploring And Learning The Terrain

If you want to be successful in finding that big treasure, you have to get out of the house. Bet out of the office, get away from the city. Not only will you enjoy exploring and learning your terrain, you get exercise and fresh air. Think of it like a camping trip or picnic. In fact, do that, go camping in the area you want to explore. That's what I did for over twenty years when I went treasure hunting. It was the best way to get out for the weekend and really connect this area. Driving back and forth out of town can seem overwhelming but if you plan a camping trip, you can leave Friday evening and spend all weekend there.

Many sites that I currently work on are on the average of a five to six-hour drive away from my home. I know from experience that I can't get to the site and have time, real time, to explore and get to know the area. This way, you can take your time and make it fun. Decide on a weekend you want to go. Mark it on the calendar and set it into stone. Keep the date, this way you're committing to yourself. Then, plan the route and the area you want to explore. Plenty of maps and satellite imagery will help you with this. Choose a good flat, open campground, not a paid campground. Remember if you want to find something that is truly lost, you need to become lost yourself.

Then decide, do you want to take your family, or friends? I suggest that you take someone with you that you can trust. It's safer so you can look out for each other and you get good company as you're out there. Not to mention, a second pair of eyes which is important. Now that you have that covered, make a supply list. What are you going to need to go camping for the weekend? I'll list a few basics below.

- Tent
- Sleeping Bag or Bedding
- Food
- Hiking Shoes
- Prescribed Medications
- First Aid Kit
- Matches or Lighter
- Ax
- Water
- Ice Cooler

Those are just the necessities. You want to become prepared. Don't go skimpy, but don't pack too heavy either. Make sure your list is good. Check it twice. Follow these instructions and I think you will be just fine. It's an adventure to see what happens.

Now that we have the basics out of the way, let's get to the real point of this chapter. This type of treasure hunting will not work in your favor if you don't know the terrain. You may have to camp at the spot several times before you find anything. You have to be tough and ready to take on off-trail hiking. Don't let this stop you.

I guarantee that if there's a hidden treasure or lost history in your area, it's because it's not easy to find. If you take a hiking trail that thousands of people have taken before you, chances are that there's not a hidden treasure waiting for you. Geocaching may work that way but not treasures that were valuable. These treasures can often be in hard to reach places. The biggest reason I suggest learning the area is because I've learned that once you get to know the rivers, canyons, hill tops in your area, you will start to see things that are man-made. Sometimes even your subconscious sees it and you don't at first.

I can't tell you how many times I've explored an area, several times over and over again to wake up to a dream. These dreams of mine that I'm talking about aren't just a random dream of who knows what. These are dreams that I have when I'm actively looking in an area and my subconscious is telling me that I missed something. Many times I've written down my dream, and made note of the canyon or field in my dream and headed out to that exact location and found something very important.

Sometimes it's a structure, rock monument, or something else that is pointing the way. You see, if you are working hard and investigating a site, you will find something if you're in the right place. Sometimes if you're in the wrong place for the specific treasure you're looking for, you may find something else that you are not expecting. This has happened to me many times. So keep an eye out for anything. I take a lot of pictures. Sometimes it's a picture of a canyon at the opening or mouth. Sometimes it is an area that has several cut trees in a weird pattern. Don't be afraid to take pictures. You don't need to be a photographer or have an expensive camera, you can just use your phone's camera.

This will help you learn the terrain better and make you sure you are successful. Here's some trade secrets that will help you.

This is a very short schooling into the mining process. In order for there to be a lost mine in the area, they needed a few many keys that now are clues. Generals. They need good sources of gold, silver, iron, copper. Check your local mining records to find if there's been a mineral source or old mining claims in the area. Second is water. This is very important. Not only did they need water to live, drinking water for the miners and animals like mules and horses, they needed a good water source, and plenty of it to maintain the smelter and processing of the minerals.

Author Standing at Old Smelter and Dry River Bed

I want to show you this picture above as an example. The structure above is an old smelter. I found this smelter many years ago. I had a lot to learn about smelters at the time, and after reaching out to many people, I learned enough to use this smelter as my example. See how I'm pointing my left finger to the dry river bed? This picture was to remind me that a water source had to be close by. In this case, within a few feet from the smelter itself. To prove this was a smelter, I took mineral assays in the river bed. It came back strong in silver and that went along with the legend. Spanish silver mines. I also examined the dry river very well and I found a rock with slag on it.

I took the rock back to my house to examine it. I found it in the dry river bed, just about 15 feet from the opening of the smelter. Slag is a name for minerals that are not gold, silver, or copper, that are discarded by the miner. Once the smelter reaches 2000 degrees,

minerals melt and the precious metals separate from the worthless minerals. The miner would toss the junk minerals aside and pour the valuable minerals into a cast for making bars.

I had this rock tested and the assayer clipped a piece of the slag off this rock. The test results came back a few days later showing that silver was the main mineral on the silver. Little tiny traces of silver. So there you have it in smelters and mines when it comes to water. Look for dry or running rivers. Do not forget or discard dry rivers. Water does revert to new locations. I've seen it happen. One year a small river is running through a small ravine and seven years later, it's now running in a new ravine, down the canyon. Miners would also dam off rivers to manipulate them to run in a different direction. Keep that in mind too.

Never think that your hard work is in vain. I can tell you that it is not. You will find something that will excite you so much, you'll never stop looking from that point. It's close to what people call gold fever. Once you get a taste of it, you'll find that inspiration to keep going. Keep on the lookout for outcroppings too. Outcropping as a patch of hard rock pillars or sections that have been pushed up through the earth with time and help from volcanic activities. This process takes thousands of years to create these outcroppings. Minerals such as gold, silver, copper, iron and many more are embedded into these outcroppings. The old miners looked for these types of things. If there were minerals found in or by the outcropping, they would start mining to see what they have found.

Here's another thing that will help you and it's a trick that I use today, all the time. When you find anything of interest, structures, symbols, mines, and anything you deem as clues, mark it on your GPS, immediately. Make sure you give your GPS a good 5 minutes to power up, and make sure it's connected to several satellites before you mark your waypoint. Name the waypoint so you can remember what it is that you're marking. Then take a picture of it. Not just one.

Take many pictures from afar, close up, from the right and left angle. One thing should have around 8 pictures of different views if you're doing it correctly.

Now that you have been researching and exploring the area, and you have pictures and waypoints, get a 7.5-minute topographic map of that area. If you are covering a lot of ground, you may need two or even four. Transfer your waypoints to the topographic map. After time, you might start to see a pattern. This might start unveiling trail routes and more. Knowing as much as you can about the area and what you are observing is crucial. You're the scientist. You're the geographer, the map maker, the prospector, the worker bee. You're all the above and as soon as you can learn these things, the sooner you will be able to start finding things and narrowing down to your riches.

Please don't give up if you're finding clues in your area. It's okay to take a break from it but don't get discouraged. Keep your records and move on to another site if you need to. How do you think I have files for hundreds of different sites? Yes, it's because some people pointed me in a direction but it's mostly because I find myself stuck at a location, without finding new clues and I leave it where it is, and move to another location. I don't typically do this for too long but as I start exploring a new or different site, it keeps me busy, doing what I like to do. It's okay to have several sites and it's okay that a site is taking a year or even four. Just keep records, maps, pictures, and waypoints.

Do what you need to do to stay positive and move in the right direction. If you like hunting for lost treasures and history as much as I do, it'll all work out for you. I believe you will be happier in life because you found and you're working on something that's different from the daily grind of work and responsibilities. That being said, if you want to become a full-time treasure hunter, do not quit your job because you think you're onto the next big motherlode. I've seen this in the past. Some people are not managing their expectations correctly. I've partnered with others before and to tell you the truth, their expectations throw a stick right in our spokes of the wheel.

After a month working with them on a project, some people can get passionate and start talking about money problems and how the treasure has to be found in the next couple weeks. They have gone on to tell me that they will lose everything if we don't find riches soon. Don't be this person. Understand that it took me over 20 years to become more flexible with money and financial responsibilities. Start off slow and make a hobby out of it. Take your time and don't mix finances with treasure hunting. If you don't have the money at the time, wait, save your money and work overtime if you can.

Then once everything is in order, you can invest in tools, equipment, and the costs of traveling and camping. You know your situation. Be smart about it. You'll be happier in the lost run. Just a side note, the partners I spoke of, do not treasure hunt anymore. They were what I sometimes call short and sweet. They treasure hunters for about one to two months. They now have a bad taste in their month. If you don't have the drive and passion for treasure hunting, you should take up a new hobby. It's only worth it if you like doing it. Let time tell you where you're going and what to do.

I promise you if you explore and get to know your area, you'll be on your way to some great adventure that you can share with your family, friends, and other treasure hunters like you.

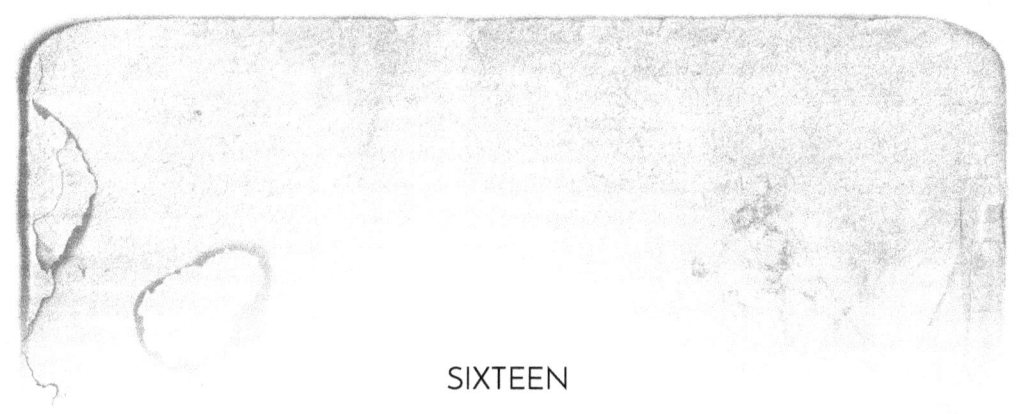

SIXTEEN

Equipment List And Personal Safety

Now let's get to the equipment that you'll need to get out there and make some discoveries. I've pondered on how to make a successful list for you. The only way I know how to do this is by breaking this section up into three different levels. I think if I create one list for beginners, a second list for immediate, and a third for advanced treasure hunters and explorers, then you can choose which one suits you best.

Here's the thing and reason why. I've been doin this for a long time. I can remember when the gear was a lot less advanced and much smaller. Then I started purchasing more and more as I went on. For a beginner, the advanced list would be overwhelming and too expensive in my opinion. It's not just about the money and costs, an advanced treasure hunter would need a lot more due to his or her activities. Let's start off with a list for beginners and go from there.

Also, you don't need the best of the best to get started. A twenty dollar backpack would work fine. A ten dollar compass and thirty dollar hiking shoes would work too. If you're new to this, take it slow. Don't break the bank. If you want to add to your list, the same goes for that too. Only choose what fits your budget. I want you to be happy and feel the excitement of becoming an adventurer. I don't want you to rack up your credit card bill just because you feel like you have to. Slow and easy as you're getting into this hobby.

You'll be happier and I would rather get positive feedback from and all the fun you are having instead of disappointments. For the beginners list, this is more of a guideline. You can buy a few things and get going on your way. You can always come back to this list and add things as you grow. At the starting point, don't worry about a tent and your camping gear.

BEGINNERS GEAR LIST

- Backpack
- Sun Protection
- Food / Snacks
- Hiking Shoes
- Flashlight
- Knife
- Camera
- Matches
- Map
- GPS
- First Aid Kit
- Rain Coat
- Water Container
- Lighter
- Sun Glasses
- Compass
- Hat

The list above will get you started. Believe it or not, this is a better list than I had. Keep it simple and lite because you're hitting the realm of a day backpacker or hiker as a beginner. Don't put a fifteen-inch knife in your backpack, that's too big and heavy. Take an actual pocket knife with you that can fit in your pocket or backpack. The one thing that you'll need more than anything is water. If you are going to go big, don't do that for water storage. You can buy a

Hydration backpack with a pouch that holds and stores your water. Make sure it's a couple of liters large. Three would even be better.

If you don't want to spend that much money on a backpack, get a few twenty-ounce water bottles and put those in your backpack. If there are disposable water bottles, that would work great. They will take some room in your backpack when they're full but one by one as you finish them, you can crush them and toss them into your bag, saving room and weight on your back. When it comes to hiking shoes, I've used cheap ones and expensive ones. I hate to tell you that no matter which ones you choose, they will only last so long. Mother nature is very hard on your shoes and hiking off trail is even worse.

I can tell you that usually what I found is, if you buy more expensive hiking shoes, your feet will appreciate it. The better shoes are more comfortable and you will be able to hike longer and feel better when you get home. Keep that in mind. If you're tough, you can go cheaper. Camera, you can use your phone for camera. That's easy. Put it in your pocket or backpack. I like mine in my backpack. That way it's not in my pocket all day after a long hike. And by the way, when I started, I hiked anywhere from three to ten miles when I went out. I wanted to cover a lot of ground. Do what your body tells you to do. Let it be your guide.

If you're looking to buy a GPS, you're going to find that if you buy them brand new, it will cost you from one hundred and fifty dollars to nine hundred. You don't need a fancy one. You can get by with the cheaper one. All you really need is to mark waypoints, that's it. The others have more options which are nice if you can afford them. Some come with a larger, color touch screen. They are very nice but you don't need them unless your pocket book allows it. Take care of it and keep it in a case in your backpack. This GPS can save you countless hours of having to go back and rediscover your discovery.

Cheap compass is fine. Later you can learn how to use a compass, laid out on the map. For beginners, you just want to know what direction you're heading. Flashlights are a big deal but they don't have to be crazy. A fifteen dollar flashlight will work just fine at first.

You can always upgrade later. Buy a small first aid kit that will fit in your backpack. Nothing too big. Just the necessities. Just like water you'll need some good food and snacks. Bring lunch and some apples, bananas, trail mix, or granola bars. They're cheap and lightweight. When it comes to a raincoat, buy the emergency ones. They're small, compacted, and cheap.

Sunglasses and hats. You will break or scratch your sunglasses or lose them at one point or the other. Your hat doesn't have to be cool. Use it to shade the sun from your head.

Now, it's time to get to the immediate adventurer's. By this time, you should have spent one to five years as a beginner. It sounds rough but that's the truth. There's no reason to buy and carry more than you can handle. If you haven't spent a while in the wilderness, then you're not ready for this list. By now, you should be savvy on structures, symbols, and how to do the trade. You should feel comfortable in your skin and start to feel confident in your decisions. You're not an expert so be careful with their states of mind but you are doing well. Because of this experience that you have, it's time to move on to bigger and better things.

It's time to upgrade and expand your list. Even the amount of days you spent looking for treasure on each trip. This is where you should be loading your vehicle with camping gear and the gear I listed above for beginners. It's time to really consider how far you want to take this. Some of you will be fast learners and some will fall behind. That's okay. It's not a contest and I guarantee you that now one will judge you on your performance. Do you think people are watching your every move when you're off-trail and four miles into the backcountry? Absolutely not.

Congratulations for getting this far by the way. It was hard work but it should feel worth it by now. I'm going to add a lot more to your list because I know you can handle it and it will only help you be more successful. The Beginners List above, you should have those things and make sure if you lose them and need to replace them that you do. You'll always need them so keep them around. The list below will be an addition to that list. I will wear you, this list may seem big and expensive but again, you don't have to have all of it at once. Take your time and start making a life change if you feel that you're ready for it. It's going to be a shocker compared to the list above.

Pretty much what you're doing is intertwining a list from a day hiker, a camper, and a treasure hunter. You'll go out and explore by day and sleep at camp at night. You want a good rest so you can be ready for the next day. Trust me, after a day, you'll be tired and every day you stay out in the field and at camp, you'll become more and more tired. I tell everyone that the rule of thumb is, if you go for a day, it'll be a day's rest once you get home. If you go for three days, you get three days of rest at home.

Here's another thing that I didn't think about until I had some experience. If you live in a city that is three-thousand feet in elevation and go to seven-thousand feet in elevation, you'll feel it. It takes about a day for your body to adjust and that means in camp and at home. The air will be thinner then you are used to so breathing and hiking might slow you down. This has been my personal checklist for several years now. I know it will help you.

- Four Wheel drive
- Insect repellent
- Metal detector
- Tent
- Big ice cooler
- Drone
- Sleeping bag
- Chain saw
- Gold Pan
- Cot or pad
- Cooking utensils
- Assay tubes
- Camping Chair
- Eating Utensils
- Camping accessories
- Ax
- Paper Plates

- Binoculars
- Shovel
- Plastic Spoons
- Stuff sacks
- Lantern
- Jacket
- Folding Table
- Hammer
- Extra clothes
- Food for several days
- Stove

When I mention four-wheel drive, this can be a SUV, UTV, ATV, or truck. You'll need something that can get you out of the mud, snow, and of the rough terrains. Even hunting after old ghost towns, you'll find yourself in need of a more aggressive vehicle. Keep in mind how much cargo you have. Trucks are the easiest due to the bed of the truck. SUV's do pretty good because you can always fold down the back seat for more room. I prefer that SUV for a couple of reasons:

1. Your cargo and belongings will not get wet if it rains.
2. If you're traveling and you stop at a store or restaurant, you can lock your SUV and not worry about someone stealing your gear.
3. SUV's do better in the mud and rough terrain because it's heavy in the rear end. Trucks tend to spin their tires a lot because the bed of the truck is actually very light. Getting up the mountain is all about traction. Aggressive all-terrain tires are a plus.

Tents to be honest with you are all about opinion. I prefer to buy a big tent so I can keep my gear inside with me to keep it out of the weather. Here's something to think about. If the package on the tent says "Four man tent," understand that they're only accounting for the room of people in sleeping bags. If I was sleeping in a one man tent, I wouldn't be able to fit my gear inside it. When I go out and sleep in a tent by myself, I use a four man tent. Sleeping bags are also what you prefer. Check your weather and temperature before leaving on your trip. If the nights drop below 50 degrees, a cheap thirty dollars sleeping bag will not keep you warm. I prefer a sleeping bag that will keep you warm to thirty degrees. This way if I have a hotter night, I can unzip it and be comfortable. If you're cold and your sleeping bag isn't keeping you warm, you're in for a long night.

Cod and sleeping pad aren't a necessity. This is for comfort only. When I was in my twenties and thirties, I used a camping pad. Now that I'm over forty, I use an air mattress. One that has a built-in pump that I can plug into my vehicle. I sleep well at night. I know how important it is to have a good night's sleep so I can be refreshed and ready to hunt the next day. Camping chairs are something that help during the evening but a log would work to sit on too. Any sharp ax will work. You'll need this for campfire wood at night and many times for fallen trees, blocking the dirt road to your campsite.

A lantern is something that is nice for night when you have to go to the bathroom and when you need to light up your tent. It can be propane or battery powered. Propane lanterns are much, much brighter but they get very hot and not suggested for inside your tent. I like a folding table, even if it's small. When I'm cooking it becomes a work table. When I want to lay out the map, it becomes my office. Food is so important. Start with making a list.

- How many days are you going to be gone?
- How many people are going with you?

Keep in mind that you need to eat good foods that provide energy. At the same time, you're gonna want to feel at home in your evenings. Be smart about it and bring plenty of food. This should be one of your top priorities. I feel that I don't have to mention it but Insect repellent is a must. Don't get bitten all day by mosquitoes and other bugs. I will make you miserable. Ice cooler, I'm going to bring my experience on this. I use top of the line coolers because even the coolers between a hundred to hundred and fifty only will keep ice for 2 days. Don't listen to the label on the cooler.

I use top brands and even then Ice will stick around for three days but the water in the cooler will stay cool for four to six days. I've used many coolers in my day. You can make the decision based on your budget. If you have an ax, you don't need a chainsaw. I went for 10 years without one but you do need an ax. Chainsaws are fun and save a lot of energy, that's for sure. What you need for cookware depends on you. Are you going to use a camping stove or cook a tin-foil dinner in your campfire? If you use a stove, I would buy a cooking set. It'll come with a couple different sizes of pots and frypans.

Same goes with plastic ware and plates. I like paper plates and paper cups, plastic silverware too. You can throw them away in the garbage and never worry about washing your dishes. Some people like the plastic set of plates and cups. You decide what you like. The hammer is for a couple things. You can use it to break rocks that may have minerals inside and you can use it to pound your tent stakes into the ground. Bring one, you'll be glad you did. Stove is up to look. Like I said, are you cooking tin-foil guy or girl or do you want to cook on a propane camping stove? When it comes to metal detectors, there's many different brands and models. Understand that there's different categories as well. All-purpose, gold, relics, beach, and underwater metal detectors. There's even deep seeking metal detectors for caches that are deeper than fourteen inches in the ground.

They can be expensive. Here's another thing, all detectors will find all metals in the ground. Not all metal detectors are waterproof. Some metal detectors only detect targets up to twelve inches in the ground. A beach metal detector is programmed to work in salt water and the others are not. A gold detector is programmed and designed to find gold that non gold detectors will miss. Treasures in America online store can help you choose what metal detector is right for you. I suggest you purchase a drone and learn how to use it. You can start off with a cheaper one at first. I would suggest staying between the two hundred and up category. I use a drone that I know has three thousand dollars invested into it.

All you need to start is one with a camera and easy to use. A drone will save you time and you would be surprised with what you can find when you have eyes in the sky. Don't buy a cheap one online that doesn't have good reviews. Buy a ten- or twelve-inch gold pan. There are many videos online to learn the basics within a few minutes of watching. This way you can follow the minerals at your site. You may find a good deposit of gold, I did. The price of gold is very high and it's a fun thing to learn. Bring some glass or plastic tubes about four inches long and one in half inches wide. If you find minerals, you can put the samples in the tube and mail it off to your closest assayer.

You'll learn what camping accessories are after a few times of going out. I would write down what you notice you need while out in the field and buy them for next time. This comes with practice. Get a good pair of binoculars. Wear them around your neck or inside your backpack when you're exploring. If you're doing it right, you'll use them several times a day. They are perfect for looking at hill tops and looking for cave/mine openings in the area. Start collecting stuff bags and duffle bags. It's perfect for putting your equipment in and traveling. Mornings and nights are going to be the coldest. During the day you might be in a t-shirt but at night, you usually need a light or heavy jacket.

Always bring extra clothes. Not only one extra step per day but extras. I've gotten wet from resin, crossing rivers, and other unaccepted mother nature related situations where I was glad that I did. You will be too. Be smart out there and take care of you and your loved ones. I've known more people that have died from mother nature and accidents than treasure hunters doing their thing.

Always tell someone that you trust where you're going and when you should be back. Give them a map of the area and where to plan to explore. Give them the location of where your campsite will be too. This way if you're not back by that time, this trusted person can get help and send out people to search for you. Search and rescue is very expensive so if you decide to stay longer, let that person know.

Every night call someone to tell them you are okay and what your activities have been. Where you have been hiking and your plans the next day. This is what has killed many treasure hunters in the past. Getting lost or hurt in the wilderness. Be careful and respect the great outdoors or it will, and I repeat, it will bite you back and you're not going to like it. Here's another very, very, very important thing. Stay hydrated and cool during the day while you're hiking around. Even in camp, stay in the shade. Dehydration and heat exhaustion are no joke. You'll die if you don't drink water. You'll burn more than twice the calories you're used to. Your energy levels and mental state will also need twice the attention. You'll most likely burn three times the calories too.

Be careful out there. I only want to hear about good things from you, not bad things. Keep a cool head and use common sense. You'll be just fine if you do and the only thing that will happen is you'll have a blast and become a great treasure hunter.

When it comes to you veteran treasure hunters, I am glad you're in this category! By now, you have proved that you are not only ready but you're devoted. This section is for those of you that have been treasure hunting for five plus years. If you're not in this category, that's okay. Keep reading and it'll give you the information you need in the future. It'll also help you prepare for what's coming. By now you should be very good at tracking down treasures and lost history. I bet you could share a lot of stories and adventures with me. The lists above should aways to your concern but I'm going to help you get even better.

Starting off, if you don't have a team and people you go out with yet, I suggest you start working on that. Take it from me, I wouldn't be where I am without a good set of friends and treasure hunters that come with me every time. Find a mixture of people with different talents and things that they're good at. It will only strengthen your team. Make sure you can trust them with your research. If you can't share your secrets with them, it will only hold you back. It's time for you to really start thinking about a big legend now. You have come this far and you have a lot of experiences, go after the mother lode. Take your team and all your equipment and do it. This can be the highlight of your expeditions.

You have most of the gear already but it's time to trade up. Go bigger and better. It will matter in the long run. Your four-wheel drive may need to be replaced soon. It's time for a bigger investment. Do you need a bigger vehicle for your gear? Most likely you do. If you're going to buy another, buy one that will fit your needs as of now. Keep in consideration more growth in the future. If you can, it's time to think about not only an aggressive truck or SUV, you need to consider buying a trailer and UTV. A side by side vehicle will go much further into the wilderness than any SUV or truck. You can cover miles and miles within a matter of a few minutes. It's time to trade in your cheaper drone and start looking at one that can fly higher and go longer. One that has 4k imaging on it. It's time to check your gear and make a list.

- Do you still have the necessities?
- Is it time to replace broken and worn out gear?
- Is it time to go bigger?

I bet you could have answered yes, yes, and yes on those questions. Maybe it's your tent. You may need to replace it or maybe even go larger. Sleeping bags get worn out after many times of using them. Think about that. It's best you pull out all your gear. Look for broken and worn out equipment. Consider if you need more, less, bigger, and/or better. The list below will have suggested gear to replace and/or trade up on. Get ready for the big show because you're in it. You're the real deal and it's going to get more interesting and exciting from here.

- UTV—Two to Four Passenger
- UTV Trailer
- Better Metal Detector
- Better Drone
- New Camping Gear
- Prospecting Tools

- New Vehicle with Aggressive Tires

Look at the different models on the market. I'm not going to lie to you, these are expensive. One can easily cost you twenty-five thousand dollars brand new. You can buy used, and I suggest that, if your budget doesn't fit a new one. Decide if you need two passengers or four. Some come with five or six. Decide if you want the sportier one with a small bed or a bigger one with a larger bed. It does matter what your cargo looks like while you're out. There's many benefits to buying a UTV. Not only will you cover more ground faster than your full sized vehicle. (SUV or truck) you'll save the wear and tear on it.

I drive my SUV up to my basecamp (campsite) and I leave it there from that point on. After unpacking and setting up camp, I use the UTV to get me and my crew around. Your truck or SUV will thank you. These vehicles are around five thousand pounds while a UTV is around twelve hundred. The suspension on a UTV is much better than on a full size vehicle. You will travel more than twice as fast and clover way more ground. UTV can go down narrow trails that full size vehicles cannot. It's a huge game changer. While you are on the market for a UTV, you'll also need to find a trailer that suits it well. These trailers are from one thousand dollars to around three thousand dollars. I'm excited for you, you are not only going to be more successful in the field, you'll have a lot more fun, trust me. It's time to trade up that old drone. You can sell it if you want or keep it as a spare.

I would say start looking at the five hundred to two thousand dollar drone. These will be all you need. Make sure you buy a trusted brand and a model that has a lot of five star reviews. Consider the options, flying time per battery, and how user friendly it is. It's time for you to learn how to be a miner forty-niner. Buy several different size gold pans and accessories. Get a ten and fifteen-inch pan. If you find a good kit, get that. It'll have everything you need. That metal detector you have been using, that should go on the shelf as an extra now. Buy a bigger and better one. If you prefer the gold detectors, go more.

It will be better for finding small and big gold pieces. Same with underwater, all-purpose, beach, and relic detectors. If you already have a deep seeking detector, consider a nothing one like an all-purpose detector. Good detectorists have two or more. I use two different kinds every time I detect. Check all your camping gear and make sure it's still functioning. If your tent has a hole in it and you're tired of getting wet during a rainstorm, buy a new one. Check all your camping gear to see what you need to replace. Your vehicle is going to be important at this point. You still need a four-wheel drive, even with a UTV. It'll still come in handy during bad weather and rough terrain.

It may be the only thing that gets you, your team, and your gear home. Consider how much it can tow. How many passengers you can carry, and the cargo space. This is your baby now. You'll learn to love it because it gets you to and from A and B. Take care of it and it'll take care of you. Some people don't understand tires but I do. Do you know I went through eight tires in two years because of the sharp rock terrain I was traveling on? I won't do that again. Now I buy mud terrain and/or all terrain tires. The walls of the tires are thick and they don't get punctured as easily. And another plus side is, the tire patterns are much more aggressive. This will give you better traction in the mud, snow, and dirt roads.

I hope this chapter helps point you in the right direction and guides you through the process. Safety is first so be careful but have fun.

SEVENTEEN

Rock Monuments And Written Inscriptions

There's all kinds of clues that can be found in the wilderness. Most of them do not have an obvious neon sign pointing right to the hidden loot or mine. The best way to find something that is lost is to understand who placed it there and when. If an ancient culture from six hundred and older built a structure or left clues around, it's like they used stone. It can be inscriptions carved in stone, stone structures, and stone monuments. There's even more than that but these are good examples and are more common in America.

When you think of Aztec or Maya structures, what comes to mind? Stone pyramids, and housing. These structures were made solely on rock. They may have had a technique with more minerals than rocks but what we see today is stone structures. They carved many hieroglyphs in stock as well. This was the ancient way and luckily for us investigators, rock lasts for thousands of years. If not even longer. The structures, carved symbols, and monuments will not live that long.

Of all the rock monuments and structures I've been involved with, people have not been able to prove that they are more than two thousand years old. Hieroglyphs will decay in a shorter amount of time. Weather and temperature is hard on them. Many different cultures and time periods made their rock monuments slightly differently. Take the Spanish as an example. They tend to build their rock monuments taller and more round at the top. Native ancient cultures leaned more to creating rock monuments with shapes. Miners build rock monuments in the shape of a triangle.

That being said, none of that really matters until you find one and start to investigate around the area. You need to find more than a rock monument to understand who built it and when. Here's another example. If you found a five-foot rock monument at a site, then searched around in the high mountains and started finding symbols on trees. You now have two different references to go off from. Then let's say that you finally find a mine opening and you inspect it. After some time, you discovered iron tools in the mine.

Now you have three points to reference and you have the style of the rock monument, the symbols carved in the tree, and you found a mine with tools. You can compare all three with information from this book. Does it look like it's from an ancient culture? Does it look like the Spanish were in the area? Or does it seem like it's from the gold rush era? I'm going to share some pictures with descriptions along with them. This may help you in your journey of discovery. In this case, you're the investigator and you need to make that judgment call by the evidence you've found in the wilderness.

Take this rock monument for example. It is only about three feet tall from the ground to the top of the monument. It doesn't appear round at the top like a Spanish monument. It's not built like a miner's marker like a staked claim marker. If you ask me, it does seem a little recent. Maybe modern, but there's a trick to this monument. There's a clue and I want you to see it up close. Look at the lichen grown on the rocks. Lichen is the mossy type growth you find on trees and rocks. Here's an interesting thing about lichen. It grows and dies. If this same rock monument suddenly appeared in a different area, the lichen would die and then start to grow again over time.

Let's say someone built this moment over 100 years ago. They found the rocks about a hundred feet from where it sits today. They took the frock from under a shaded tree and placed them here. The lichen that was growing under the tree on the same rocks, would die. This is because the rocks had shade and when it rained, the tree kept some of the rain off the rocks. Now they're in the sunlight, without shade. This would have killed the original lichen and now what you see today is the new lichen since it's been moved and built. Same rocks, but now it's in a new environment.

I can tell you that this color of lichen growth, bright orange and dark black are different types of growth. The black is older than the orange. It's hard to get a date on it but I can tell you that the bright orange can be as old as five hundred to one thousand years. Because of the black lichen, it could be even older. It could be a couple thousand years old. It so far seems that someone built this over a few hundred years and I would say that it appears to be a more native type built then the Spanish.

I walked through the area when this rock was found. I found over a hundred other rock monuments. All of them had lichen that suggested about the same time frame, five hundred to thousands of years old (could be older, like I mentioned above, due to the black lichen. These other rock monuments have spades and different sizes to them. At this point, I think it's safe to say that the Spanish didn't build them. It's hitting the time frame when it would be too soon for the Spanish to be in the middle north American area. It's too old to be from a miner in the 1800s and it's way too old to be a hiker's cairn.

I would say that this area and monuments belong to the people that have lived here for thousands of years. Native Indians. That's just judging a book by its cover. Yes, we have a rough estimated time stamp, but it's not as normal for the natives in the last thousand years to build rock monuments like the other hundred that I saw. It could be safe to think that these monuments may have belonged to ancestors of the native Indians we think of today. Although this is just a clue or speculation based on a rough date of the lichen. I have not spent more time in this area. If I did, I would be looking for more clues that could help me understand who built them.

This rock monument is what we call a "Window Monument." These are extremely helpful when it comes to direction and even distance. With a window rock monument, not only should you feel like you are narrowing down your search to an area, you should be excited to see where to go next. The window monument can tell you many things about when it was possible to be constructed by the lichen and it should tell you where you need to go next. This window monument has four windows in it. Do you see them? The four hallowed squares that you can see through.

These are clues. In my experience, it doesn't matter who built them, these windows are not just a design, there is a picture frame for you to see where to go. All you need to do is put your face up against the window opening and see what you see. Once you have that picture frame view, with your face against a rock monument, see what you see.

Is there another rock monument in the frame? Is there a hilltop or mountain peak in the frame?

This is what you need to decipher. It's going to take trial and error to unravel this mystery. Unfortunately, this window monument has four windows. Four openings that point to different locations. That means you're going to have to travel to these four places to find more clues. If all four may point to the same place, you are pretty much in luck. That means that the creator is reassuring you that it's definitely pointing to a place of importance. There is no guesswork to that. Go to where the window is pointing.

Another thing to look for inside the window is a small marker or pointer. This could be made of rock or wood. This pointer is a way to use it as a sight, like a gun. If the window has a pointer inside the window, close one eye and see what it's pointing to. I guarantee that it's very important. If you look closely to the left of the top (first) window, you can see that it does have a pointer inside the window. After careful inspection, I could see that it was pointing to the top of the mountain in the distance. Not just any mountain top but to a very strange looking peak that sticks out from the rest.

We did inspect the lichen and it suggested that this monument was built over one thousand years ago. This is exciting because now we know to look for markings and clues that point to ancient people. After doing some research, local people that live in this area talk about history that belongs to an ancient tribe, not names or recorded in any history books. Local legends say that ancient people lived in the area for thousands of years and they had a place where they stored all their prized treasures, written language on stone tablets, and even a burial site of the kings and queens. Does this sound too farfetched? Don't be so fast to judge a local legend. I've learned in the years of treasure hunting that there's a little bit of truth to every legend.

Hieroglyphs Carved into Stone Taken by Author

The hieroglyphs in the picture above are from the mountain top that the window monument pointed at us too. Strangely these hieroglyphs are not by the strange peak that I spoke of but on the other side of the mountain. The distance between the monument and these hieroglyphs are about fifteen miles away. I've been to this site many times but I know for a fact that I haven't found all the clues. In fact, I believe I may have missed some in between the monument and the hieroglyphs. The reason I think that is because of two factors.

1. Fifteen miles seems to be a long distance for one clue to lead to other clues, without something else in the middle of that. I still believe today that I need to go back to the strange looking peak and look harder. I think I missed something.
2. The monument points to the strange looking peak, not the back side of the mountain. I think whatever this monument is pointing to is where the treasure and lost history really is. This site is a great example to you so you know, never give up. Always look for more clues.

This site is still being investigated by my team and I. I will not disclose the location. If I make a discovery, I will let the public know. The hieroglyphs in the pictures above have still not been explained. Some local historians think they know what it is and what it might say but I think I know better. They're not taking in account for the hundred plus rock monuments of the other side. Another thing is they don't mention the different types of mixed cultural symbolism, written in these hieroglyphics.

It was very common for ancient people to inherit languages from each other. This goes for building similarities, written language, and more. I think this panel of ancient writing is only two things.

1. It's a hoax and someone thinks they're cool for creating it.
2. The hieroglyphs do belong to an unknown ancient people

At this point, I can't not say. I will not give my opinion on that yet. I will never say something is or is not something without more evidence. This can throw someone else off course. It could contaminate their research. No matter what, one thing for sure. The rock monuments and hieroglyphs and an amazing discovery. It could possibly change history as we know it. There's no reason to rush to a decision and be quick to brand something. Time and research will uncover its mystery.

Side note: When you find hieroglyphs like these above, read them from right to left. Ancient people wrote this way. Even if you knew what it said, it wouldn't make sense unless you start from the first line, from the right, and read it from there.

The following picture is what I found several years ago. I think this story may help you in your journey. I was at work one day, sitting at my computer in my office. A man that I realized came into my office and asked if he could shut the door to talk. After he shut the door, he sat down in the chair across from me and told me a story that was right up my alley. He started off by explaining he noticed talk around work that I was known as a treasure hunter. I acknowledged that he was correct. He then looked at the wall to the left of him and saw some of my pictures and discoveries I've found in the past.

Rock monument hidden behind brush

I think he was sizing me up. He hesitated for a moment, then started off like this: "There's a legend around where only old timers talk about. I'm going to tell you this because I'm moving to Florida and I have no reason to come back. If you go to Veyo, Utah, and find the mountains to the west, you'll find a peak that is made of solid granite."

He went on to tell me that the first settlers in the area heard from the local Indians that a massacre took place at the granite mountain top. He said that many people have been looking for a gravesite of the eight Spaniards that were buried there. The Indians abused them and buried them with all their belongings. He then said that there should be an old mine that the Spanish worked for about five years. They used the Indians as slaves and that's why they killed them. I could tell by his eyes that he at least believed what he told me.

He mentioned that he had been up there several times to look for clues but was unsuccessful. I then asked him if he could show me this area on a map. He agreed. He pointed to the mountain peak, made of granite. I wasn't more than three weeks later, I entered the area with a friend of mine. We took two ATV's (four-wheelers) to the area. The thing that got me excited was he was right so far. The mountain pearl he showed me on the map was definitely made of solid granite. My friend and I found gold flakes with our metal detectors in a canyon close by. We decided to head down the trail a little more for about three miles. That's where we found this rock monument.

If you look at the picture above, you can see the old monument in the vegetation. This picture was taken just a few feet away from the trail. My four wheeler is right behind me. What you see in the picture above is what our eyes saw. I knew that it was going to be something great. As I approached it, I took another picture which is the picture below. When I started to investigate the monument, I noticed that the lichen seemed to match the time period. I was told in the late 1700s. I think that could match this monument. I also noticed the pointer rock at the top of the rock monument. It seemed to be a directional pointer. Tell me where to go.

We didn't find the mine. We did follow the pointer to another monument, then another monument. I have no reason to not believe the legend at this time. Everything the man told me was true. I have a trip planned for a few months from now. Using satellite imaging, I think I may have found a disturbed area that could be a mine, just about one mile away.

The rock monument is old. You can clearly see the lichen and the pointer on top of the rock in the following photo. It doesn't seem to match what I've seen of ancient monuments, made by ancient people. It doesn't seem to match a mining claim marker from the 1800s. I can tell you that it's not from a hiker, creating a cairn so they can mark their trail. I believe this is a Spanish marker (monument). I think it is pointing the way to their lost mine.

I did check mining records and nothing came back for this area in the 1800s or 1900s. I don't believe it's that recently made. I can tell you this, if you look close enough at the pictures above, the rock monument seems to be on its last leg. It must have been built when the brush (vegetation) was that thick. We had to push several bushes out of our way to get to it, and it's only ten feet from the trail. This matches everything that I've seen in the past to an official Spanish rock monument.

I did a little more digging and found out that the trail we used has never been made into a road. It's always been a small horse trail according to the Forest Service. A Spanish monument next to an old horse trail is typical. If a rider saw this in the old days, they would have to figure out what it meant and where it was pointing to. This is why we didn't find the mine that day. It was supposed to stay hidden. My friend and I were there all day long and we didn't see anyone around. Not one person, dirt bike, ATV. The forest service was surprised that we made it that far. It was a rough little trail. The Forest Service built wood pillars from all four sides of the area so only ATV and bikes could enter the area. We traveled twenty miles of this rough little trail to get to the area.

This is why I say, keep your eyes peeled. You never know what you're going to find. Remember this as well, the terrain changes all the time. What it looked like to us a few years back, was differently different than it looked in the late 1700s. Never figure that something is going to be easy to find.

EIGHTEEN

Conclusions And Final Thoughts

In every party, group, community, and organization, there needs to be a voice that stands up for others. Treasure hunting has been looked at as a group of people that break the law in America. Selfless people that go out to seek personal gain. I want to change that idea. Many states in America have many laws and regulations in each county and in their state. These laws hold back many types of legal, or too slim, options for a treasure hunter. The impression I get is lawmakers think it will stop all the looting. It doesn't! I guarantee you treasure hunting and historical research is just like every other situation around the world. There's good people and bad people in every group and community.

The bad people tend to ruin it for the good people. The treasure hunters that do this type of work for personal gain will continue doing it. Laws, regulations, and moral values don't stop them. It only holds back the law-abiding citizens. Here's an example: in Europe there have been many discoveries of old medieval relics, pirate caches, Viking treasures and many more discovered in their country. One thing that separates them from us is these parts of Europe offer a finder's fee to the treasure seeker. They work together and no one goes to jail for a discovery, as long as they do it according to the laws. Seventy percent of the discoveries in Europe are found by treasure hunters, scholars, and hobbyists.

The finder gets their name put on the discovery and terms of a finder fee is negotiated. I believe if the United States rewrites our treasure hunting laws, similar to other countries, many more discoveries will be made in America. It should stop some and even a lot of the legal looting in America as well. This idea, other than small cases, has never been taken to the courts. No one knows how to attack or approach this type of concern. Can you imagine what kind of discoveries would come out in the public if our states will work with us? Did you realize that hundreds of artifacts and lost historical history is hidden from the public due to these laws and fear of someone being prosecuted?

It would be a big change but it will not happen until we get organized and work together. In all my years of treasure hunting, I've seen and noticed the treasure seekers in America. I'm friends with a lot of them and we try to work together as much as possible. The thing that I've noticed and this is what I think keeps our community divided is being noticed. If you go on social media, you can find thousands of people who metal detect, treasure hunting, gold panning, ghost town exploring, and mining. That's just mentioning a few groups out there. My companies did a lot of research years ago to see how big the treasure hunting community is.

To our surprise, we found over a hundred and fifty thousand, just on one social media platform. My companies also spent time on what is called SEO (Search engine optimization) to find the keywords and how many people are searching these types of terms every month. Again

To our surprise, we collected this information below. Each number is per month. How many times these words have been typed and searched in a search engine every single month.

Keywords for Related Web Searches

- Metal Detecting – one hundred and fifty thousand
- Metal Detectors – one hundred and sixty thousand
- Ghost Towns – six hundred thousand

- Adventures – eight million
- Treasure Hunting – three hundred thousand
- History – eight million, five hundred thousand

This is only naming and displaying over five thousand keywords we researched. We figure that there are over five hundred thousand active treasure hunters online, every month. We also discovered that there are over five million people interested in treasure hunting. These are big numbers. It proved to me and others that many people are either treasure hunting themselves or they are interested in treasure hunting. Take a look around and see how many tv shows are now playing about treasure hunting, gold mining, and unsolved mysteries around the world. Look how Hollywood is creating good movies based around treasure hunting.

This is not a small community and it is not short on attention. Now, many others like myself are trying to make their names stick out. This means competition for everything. Books, social media, videos, and more. Our community is divided because many of us are in a compilation for likes, views, and attention. I realized this about two years ago and from there, I decided to not post on social media as much. I decided to let other tools become my voice. If this community came to find a group of leaders and move forward towards getting some of these laws changed, I think we can make a difference.

We can still have our own platforms and websites but work together to educate the world that history is being destroyed, looted, and hidden from us. I don't know the first steps on how to go about it. I can only tell you what I've seen throughout the years. For those of you that like to see and hear about treasure hunting, that's great too. You equal a bigger percentage than the treasure hunters actually doing the field work. Entertainment, curiosity, and hobbies are a big deal and that's why I am mentioning this subject in my first book. I want to make everyone I can aware of the ins and outs of treasure hunting and historical researching.

I'll tell you what. I'll show one more thing in this book. One more thing and a quick story that I think will make you become even more of a believer in lost history. There's so much of it. I get connected every day with a new possible discovery. Most of them come from right here, in North America. So about ten years ago I was contacted by a friend of a friend who told, I know about historical artifacts and lost history. He started off by being secretive and slow to get to the point. He seems nervous and scared to tell me something that was on his mind.

After some time of convincing him that he was safe to tell me his story, he told me a good one. I'm going to conceal his name and location at this time, but I will explain the story and details. He told me that he and a family member were in the wilderness exploring and hiking around, not more than ten miles out of his town. To make a long store shorter, they found a cave opening and decided to venture into it. Within about a hundred feet inside the cave, they noticed strange writings with blue and red colors on the wall. They decided to follow that rest of the cave to see what they could find. About four hundred feet inside the cave, they came to the end of it. One of them noticed that there was a cutout, a carved shelf in the wall.

They noticed that there was some type of black like ash under the shelf, almost as if a fire was burning in a controlled way for a long time. One of them used their flashing to look on top of the shelf. It was carved about two feet into the hard rock wall. They found an artifact in the picture above. Now this man was scared of getting into trouble with the law. He was warned by treasure hunters before me that the government will take it from you and charge you with the antiquities law. Lucky for him, I had a friend that was an archaeologist. Once I called him, we put the artifact in his hand and he stayed in communication with us.

We all sat down for a meeting at a restaurant to hear the story and talk about the next steps. The pictures are from that meeting. After a few months, reports started to come in. The artifacts were passed around a few universities for the studying process. We did find out that the artifact was about five hundred to six hundred years old. Putting it around the mid-1500s. The origin of the artifact resembled that of Central America. Some said similar cultures like the

Aztec, Maya, & Mixtec people. But no one could agree with it because it has similarities but is different.

We were told that it appears that it may have been made in a rougher environment than a town or place where they could have taken more time on it. Almost like it was created by a culture that was on the move. Not a permitted culture that lived in the area with well-established facilities. It also appeared to them that this artifact was in a likelihood of a god. The baby in between the legs of the artifact is representing life and birth. This god and artifact would be a celebration of life. That's all we know about it. I will tell you that it was found in the lower western states of America.

In a not so obvious area. That one that you would think. The location is off any major trail that history talks about. I did some research and I found that there was an ancient road (trail) that was used by ancient natives before the Spanish Trail was named what it is today. It passed this area and headed many miles to the east and then many miles to the north. Ending around a modern little town today. This same town is known to have quite the Aztec history and legends surrounding it. I'm sure what to make of that but since then, I've been contacted about other people finding old artifacts like ancient tools and weapons around the remote area of where this god artifact was found. Here's some more pictures from this meeting.

I never did have this artifact in my position other than at the time of the meeting at the restaurant. I left that in the hands of the person who discovered it and the officials. I hope by telling you this story, you can see that discoveries are made every day. By average people. Never think you can't make a difference. Never assume you can't change history. I hope this book has helped open your eyes to different possibilities then you were aware of. My extension was to open your mind with some history you may have not heard before. I also wanted to share to you that not all things are what they seem. I also hope that you gathered that not the information you are told is correct or even a flat out lie.

I don't think it's just bad people, trying to cover up information and history. I think it comes down to a few upper end officials that have the power to control what is released and how it's released. Educated people coming out of school are all taught the same thing. I don't know if they know any better after being told what is what for years by their teachers and textbooks. Why would they? To them, people like me are wrong because they were not taught to think like that in schools, colleges, and universities. I feel the same way about their schooling. I noticed it while I was studying at university. I did take it a step further and researched on my own time, in and out of the field. What I was discovering and learning were two different things when I was learning in school. There's some food for thought.

The rest of this book below is for you. I wanted to give you more information so if you wanted to try your luck and time with treasure hunting and historical research, you have enough to go out there now. The next couple chapters will help you find and understand more about treasure hunting symbols and I left you a big treasure on the last chapter. I left you over two hundred treasure stories and legends for you to see and read about. I not only wrote a small description for every story, I left names of the people involved. I also included the locations to the best of my knowledge, including modern day names of towns and cities. Many of these stories have the value of the treasure itself that is still lost. Most of the dollar amounts are from the value of the treasure in the time it became lost.

That means you can more than eight times the value for modern day value. For example, $7,500 dollars or gold and silver in 1896 would be worth around $250,000 dollars today. That's just the increase of our current currency and the price of gold and silver today. To a collector, it can double the modern day value if you can prove it was a buried treasure, linked to a legend of the past. I hope you enjoyed my book. I hope you take advantage of the information and experiences I've given you. Use this book often to refer to rock monuments, treasure carving and symbols.

Good luck. Be Safe. Find your adventure.

NINETEEN

Using Treasure Symbols As Clues

This section of the book will show you and explain some of the symbols I've encountered in the wilderness. I want you to understand that these symbols can have many different meanings. They have been used by many different cultures, and they have been used around the world. If you find one carved on a tree or rock, know that it could have a slightly different meaning. What really deciphers the mystery of what the symbols are telling is to find more in the area and use them together as one. Use common sense and these meanings below to help you get closer to the treasure.

When it comes to symbols and treasure clues, sometimes you have to try different scenarios. If a symbol is leaning to the right or left, it may be wanting to go that direction but sometimes they are meant to throw you off course. If you follow it to the right for a mile and don't find other clues, follow it to the opposite direction.

These symbols are only a clue. Trial and error is the point of this game. What you see below are the more frequently used meanings but they are not set in stone. You as the investigator will have to try different scenarios to understand the true meaning. This can prove to be time consuming at some locations. Look at the bright side of things, you're very close to something very important if you start finding symbols.

Sometimes it can mean that you are there, looking around and sometimes you may have to continue on the same path for two to three miles. Once you find symbols, always go slow. Take your time because there might be more symbols to help. You don't want to miss those. It's easier to stay on track with clues like these. Backtracking can be confusing and it can take a lot more time. Make sure you mark every single symbol location with your GPS. You'll need those and I can guarantee that. Take it from me.

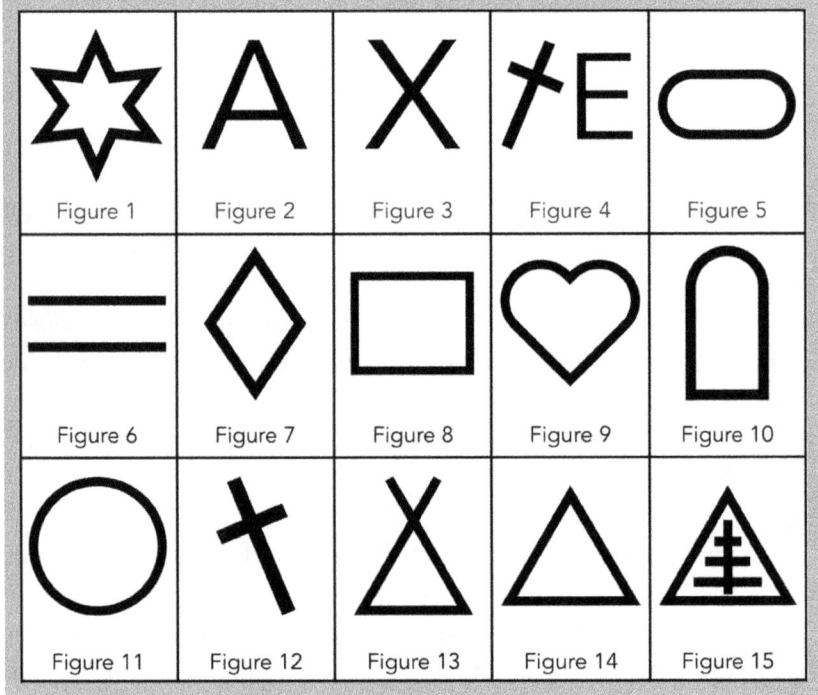

Treasures of the Ancients | 189

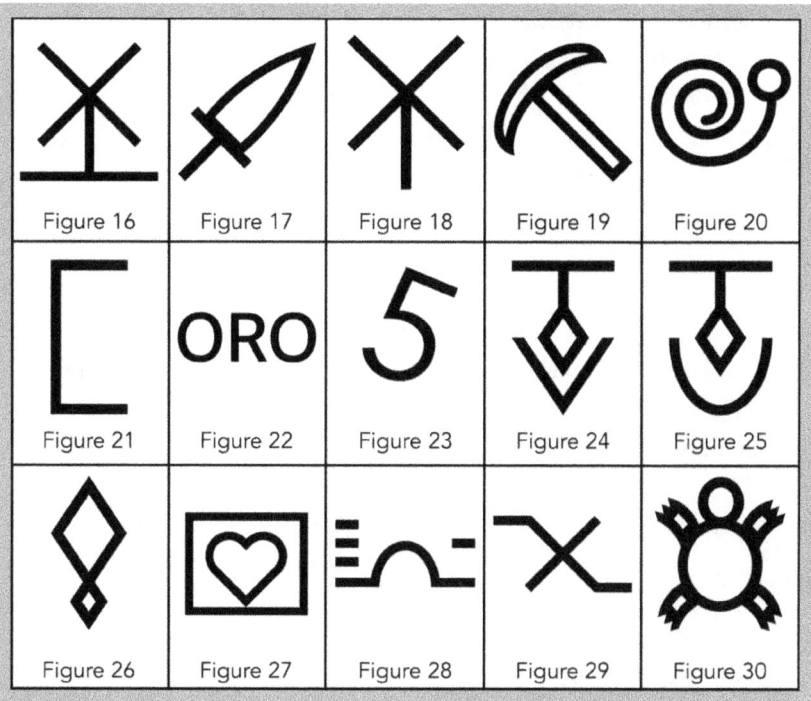

Figure 16 | Figure 17 | Figure 18 | Figure 19 | Figure 20
Figure 21 | Figure 22 | Figure 23 | Figure 24 | Figure 25
Figure 26 | Figure 27 | Figure 28 | Figure 29 | Figure 30

Figure 1—The star can be good or bad. Depending on the history of the area, it can mean *safety* or *death*. If you find this in your area, be careful until you know you're out of danger.

Figure 2—The A shaped symbol is a directional indicator. Follow the direction of the point. If the symbol is leaning to the left or right, follow that direction. If it is upside down, back track in the direction.

Figure 3—The X is a great symbol and has a few different means:
    1.) On the trail to treasure
    2.) 10
    3.) Look for Landmark
    4.) Change in Course

Figure 4—This symbol can have two meanings. It can mean "Stop" or "Turn"

Figure 5—You may want to really consider what your next move is if you find this symbol. It has several meanings.
   1. One
   2. Go to the nearby Mountain or Knoll
   3. This is the place (Look Around)
   4. A treasure belonging to the church
   5. Mine or treasure nearby

Figure 6—Know this can get a little tricky. It can be combined with the oval symbol in figure 5. If it is separated, by itself it can mean two things go double the distance or two Varas away from where you are standing.

Figure 7—This symbol has proven to be reliable and its meaning is "One League" away. One Legua (League) is 2.52 miles away in old Spanish measurements.

Figure 8—If you see this you may want to see if there's any direction or distance symbols nearby. These other symbols could be in the same place or even a few feet away. It means *Treasure*.

Figure 9—This is a marker for the Kings Mine. This means there's a rich mine very close to where you're standing.

Figure 10—If you find this it means you're looking for a hidden mine. This symbol can be found by itself or along with others.

Figure 11—This symbol means look for a cave or mine opening. Again it could be along with other symbols nearby.

Figure 12—The leaning cross can be a directional indicator and/or it can mean that the Spanish were in the area. Follow the direction of the cross and see what you find.

Figure 13—This symbol was used by the Spanish to tell another person that there's an Indian tribe in the area.

Figure 14—This means 120 degrees. It should have another symbol nearby. Something to reference a direction of distance.

Figure 15—Look towards a wooded tree line or forest. This means that a treasure will be there. Look around as you enter the trees for other symbols for direction and/or distance.

Figure 16—This meaning is simple, it's another Spanish cross. Meaning that you are now looking for something the Spanish is hiding.

Figure 17—Follow the point or direction of the dagger. It could also mean the opposite as well. Follow the point. If you need to, back track and follow the other direction.

Figure 18—This symbol means that a Mexican descendant has been in the area. Most likely a son or grandson of an original Spaniard that worked the area. This means there's been a couple generations mining or hiding treasures in the area.

Figure 19—The mining pick can mean following the direction of the pick or that you are very close to a mine.

Figure 20—If you find a coiled snake with the head, follow the direction that the head is pointing to. Most likely there will be more symbols found.

Figure 21—If you find this symbol it means that there's a mine nearby with only one entrance.

Figure 22—Congratulations. If you found this symbol it means "Gold". Look for more symbols because most likely there will be.

Figure 23—The learning five symbol means that you need to follow the way it is learning and go five varas from there. One varas = 32.5 inches. Five varas = 162.5 inches.

Figure 24—This means that there's a mine in the canyon ahead. Look in all directions for the closest canyon. You may still need to travel a bit to the canyon. It could be hidden.

Figure 25—This symbol is just like the one above but instead it tells you to look around for a valley and go there. That's where you will find a mine. It could be hidden.

Figure 26—This is a distance indicator and it could have a treasure symbol or mine symbol nearby. It means one and one-half leagues away. One Legua means 2.52 miles. This symbol would mean go 3.78 miles from where you are standing. Look for a direction indicator symbol nearby and follow it.

Figure 27—This symbol means that there's a "King's Treasure" nearby. This would be a huge treasure, very rich and valuable. Look for other symbols nearby.

Figure 28—This is a symbol for where they lived. It means living quarters. This could be a place of wood or stone structures. Sometimes just an old campsite.

Figure 29—This symbol has three meanings and all three mean stay on your toes and pay attention to more symbols. You don't really want to find this one, it can be confusing.
   1.Wrong way
   2.Change direction
   3.Return to the last symbol or clue you found

Figure 30—This one is a turtle and I don't know one experienced treasure hunter that doesn't get excited if this is found. It does have a lot of meanings. It can be found like the picture shows. Sometimes it will have no tail. It can also be missing its legs. Explanation below. Often used by the Spanish but others have used it too. Always be on the lookout for more symbols. You most likely will have a hard time finding the treasure without a direction and/or distance. They will be closed on another rock or tree nearby.

1. Main meaning is "Treasure Nearby
2. If the head is not present, that means the treasure is gone or removed
3. If the legs are missing, this means you are standing at the spot of treasure. Use a good deep seeking metal detector and scout that spot.
4. If the tail is leaning and not straight, follow that direction of the tail.
5. Always look at the body of the turtle symbol, there could be another symbol carved in it. A direction or distance is common to find on the shell.

This is a great example of what you want to find. There's two symbols present on these two trees.

1. The symbol for a mine tunnel or entrance
2. The symbol for a treasure. This turtle is intact

See how the two symbols are large and one is in front of the other? This is how you would want to find them. (Refer to Figure 30.) This turtle has the head, legs, tail, and a diamond carved into the shell which means *one legua* (league) is 2.52 miles away. (Refer to Figure 7.)

This symbol can have a few different meanings. (Refer to Figure 3.)

I'm going to show you some of the commonly found treasure clues. These symbols are very important and if you start finding some, play close attention to them. These are some of the symbols I've mentioned in this book. It takes years to understand them and sometimes, you will never fully understand but there is a great indicator that you are in the right place. If you find one, don't assume that's the only one in the area. Sometimes you may only find one. Many times there's more to be found and they will help you understand what is hidden and where.

Author at a King's Mine next to a Spanish tree symbol marking

The heart symbol belongs to the Spanish. Its meaning is very important and if you ever find one, carved in a tree or rock, you need to keep your eye out for a mine opening. Not just any mine. A king's mine which should be very rich with gold, silver, copper, and possibly other minerals. The King of Spain funded the mining process because it is a rich mine.

I want to show you this so you can see that not all the tree markings you find are in great shape. In fact, most of the symbols you find are old and decaying with mother nature. Don't take the symbol at face value. Some people will pass by a tree or rock carving and call it fake, a hoax, or too recent. After time you will notice that some look too freshly carved and some do not.

Don't assume that just because the markings look fresh, that they are. It all depends on what type of tree it is. Young trees that the Spanish marked could've been growing with the tree without the right nutrients and minerals in the ground. That can make the markings appear older and destroyed in a shorter amount of time.

This works both ways. Never could carvings look older than they really are. Many things can alter a carving on a rock or tree. Is there a lack of sunlight on the markings most of the day? Is the marking covered by something above to block the snow and rain from hitting it and weathering it faster? Pine trees in the western states are different from pine trees in the eastern states. All these things you have to take in consideration.

Don't be one of those people that so easily brand something real or fake. Then time and looking for evidence be your guide. I promise you will get the hang of it after time. Here's another thing to consider. Pine trees can grow and live past 500 years. Aspen trees can grow and live around 150 - 250 years. That can help you get an estimate of when the person who carved it did it. No one would use a young tree. They wouldn't use an old tree either. They would have looked for trees in the area that not only are close to what they hid, but healthy trees so they won't die too soon.

Author At Spanish Cross Tree Carving

It was common for the Spanish to leave their mark. A cross represents their religion. Meaning if a group of Spanish came back for a mine or a treasure after an early Spanish group left it, it was made obvious whose area it was. If you find something like this, be on the lookout. Many areas where I've been looking and hunting for lost Spanish history and treasures, I've found not only one marking but several. Many sites have had rock monuments and tree carvings. Or rock monuments and rock carving. Sometimes, they would use one location and place several in a small area and that is it. Sometimes they can spread from many miles.

Again, do not assume that all sites are the same. The symbol meaning should be roughly the same but not the exact of how the symbols were used for directing you to the stop of interest.

Follow the long arm, or flip 90 degrees then follow.

This is a triangle, carved in stone. For thousands of years the triangle has been used by many different types of people and cultures. This is a big deal because it's trying to point you in the right direction, if you can decipher it. I have not found one yet that's not linked to other clues in the area that speaks treasure or something very important.

Above you will see my notes and though this is the common meaning for this symbol, it doesn't always mean what this one says. It depends on who carved it and what they are hiding. Use the longer arm of the triangle to point you in the right direction. While you're standing at the marking, look around to see if you can see a hill or mountain in that direction. If you can, use binoculars to see if you can see a rock monument in the distance. This could save you time.

Never discard this type of carving. I promise you it has a meaning for a reason. This wouldn't have taken a few minutes to carve. This was a purposely place for something big. Never forget where you find clues like this. Mark them on your GPS and save it. Even for years to come. I've been working on some sites for years and then new evidence comes my way and I pick up my hunt where I left it.

Some people believe that this marking means water. The only problem I have with that is that I've found many of these in an area where they are very close to a water source. True water was a lifeline and like gold for survival but why place it on a cliff, just a few hundred feet from a river or stream? Some people believe it's a symbol for a bigger purpose. They call it the Key Symbol.

These are your typical native Indian petroglyphs. Some people believe they have a hidden meaning and that might be true. I have learned that many Indian tribes were telling their story. Generations of the sun and winter. The people of their tribe. Hunting and gathering. I'm not saying that they were simple people. They just cared a lot more about things that you and I take for granted.

I know a few people that are somewhat of an expert when it comes to Indian petroglyphs and pictographs. If you ever get a chance to listen to them talk at a site, do it. Don't over complicate these symbols too much as you're getting started in your research. Many people think they have cracked the code. I believe some books and websites can lead you in the wrong direction.

Take it slow and easy. Sit back and observe these petroglyphs if you come across some. Notice that many of them have pictures of animals, people, and landscapes.

Do not and I mean do not do anything to damage petroglyphs. They could be hundreds, if not thousands of years old. Remember, even the oils from your skin, just from touching them, can cause damage over time.

Authors Wife (LeeAnn Draper) Photographing The Panel

These are called pictographs. These are from natives Indians as well. This is one of my favorite places to visit. I think these are talking about life. Life on earth and the afterlife. See the centerline? This line spreads for 50 feet on this panel. If I look in the center, you will see what looks like a spaceship, blasting through a layer.

If you thought that, you're somewhat correct. I've met with the local Indian tribe and they tell me that this is somewhere between 700 and 1000 years old. They claim that it was drawn by their ancestors. In the more prehistoric times.

They explained to me that the center line represents earth, life on earth. Everything below is hell and everything above it is heaven. On this panel you can see figures of people below and above. This was a story talking about what happens when you die. Good people are reborn into a new life and people who did bad will stay underground. It seems that Indian tribes believe in something as the Christianity does as well. Or at least in the general way of speaking.

Like I mentioned in this book, the Spanish were conquered. If native Indians were in the area, it's likely that the Spanish tracked their tribe down to gain information and sometimes more. Keep that in mind when you're in an area that has Indian history. I've even seen Indian petroglyphs with Spanish carvings on the same rock. The Spanish would sometimes disguise their marking by mixing them with others.

Unfortunately, this site is much more known now than when I found them. Since then, people have gone to the site to destroy some of these pictographs. It appeared that they used large rocks to throw them at the pictures. It permanently left damage to this panel. Please educate yourself and others around you. Teenagers are definitely responsible for my choice. At least at this site. Parents tell your kids about this and let them know that we can never get history like this back once it's gone.

This next picture was taken by my daughter (Jada Johnson) when she was in Hawaii. She came back home from her vacation and told me all about these strange and beautiful markings all over the rocks. She mentioned that she found them in more than one place. Many of them were close to the beaches. I know from my research that there are many treasure sites that people claim are in Hawaii and the islands surrounding it.

If you thought only Europeans and Native America's did this type of thing, guess again. These types of writing and markings have been around for thousands of years by many cultures around the world. In this book, when you get to the last chapter, I list several treasure stories for Hawaii. If you go to Hawaii, look around and keep your eyes open. You might find some too.

Treasures of the Ancients | 203

These ruins are from my trip to Cancun Mexico. Even though this trip was more for pleasure than work, I never stopped investigating. The Maya built these many years ago. The Yucatan is holding onto many secrets that we Americans don't recognize and understand. This is a great example of what ancient ruins look like today.

I wanted to use this as an example. How old do these inscriptions look to you? They are bright white then the native Indian petroglyphs I showed a few pictures above. I did some research in the area where I found these markings. Many Indian petroglyphs can be found in the area. This one stuck out to me because it looked newer and fresher than the others.

After returning home, I did some research and learned that C.C.C was in the same area in the 1930s. They were building dams nearby to revert the water from the river. Do you think it's possible that one of the workers created this? Perhaps he or she was inspired by the Indian petroglyphs in the area. The date does match the time period of the C.C.C.

I would say that this is exactly what it looks like. Someone in 1936 knew the technique of creating petroglyphs and he or she wanted to leave their mark for everyone to see. I would say that the marking fits that and the age looks about right.

This is a smelter. The door is on the other side of the structure. Because it's on an Indian reservation, I couldn't get close enough to see if it's more from the 1800s mining era or if it's a Spanish smelter. To be honest, it reminds me of the Spanish way of building a smelter but it's in really good shape. That could be for many reasons. Because this land was granted to the local Indian tribe many years ago and they do not let any outsiders on this area of land, maybe it's been preserved after all this time.

It also could be from the old mines in the 1800s. The Spanish smelter construction was inherited by some in the old days. Some people found an old smelter from the Spanish and copied the construction and method. Many of our ancestors were from Europe at one point or another. That technique could have been brought from Europe. It's hard for me to tell without seeing it up close.

I had to zoom in my camera about 3 football fields away to get this picture. This is another example of keeping your eyes peeled for anything unnatural and man-made while you're out.

This is a completely different situation than others in this book. While my team and I were filming for the Travel Channel, we were hunting for Butch Cassidy's gold from the robbery at Castle Gate. A payroll stash that Butch and his gang, The Wild Bunch, hid deep in the Canyonlands of Utah.

The writing that you see reads, *Butch Casady*. It's misspelled. That was done with wagon grease and that does match the time period. I've found many inscriptions written in wagon grease over the years. Many believe it is a time period from the 1800s. Sometimes wagon grease was all a person had on them back then. Many Americans didn't know how to write or draw like the Indians did with petroglyphs.

If it was Butch Cassidy, why did he write his name wrong? You would like that a person would know how to spell their name. After finding this a few miles away from Robbers Roast, local people contacted me and told me that it was a code. A treasure code that Butch used. Is it possible that Butch was leaving a clue for him and his gang when they returned? This is a great question but I'm going to save this discussion for a later book. I promise I'll tell you what my team and I discovered and more.

Author Posing For Picture At Dinosaur Tracks

Dinosaur tracks in southern Utah are not that common but more common than some places. I learned about this area and decided to go find them. Since then, I learned of many more in the area about 25 miles to the north.

I used distilled water to show that footprint better. These dino tracks are not covered by the sun or weather. Nothing is stopping these tracks from disappearing with time. It is a great site and if you know of any, take care of the place or your children may never see them. Maybe it'll be your grandchildren. One thing for sure, these tracks are old and mother nature hasn't erased them yet.

Hopefully they will remain for many years to come so everyone can see them. Hopefully, the wrong kind of people won't visit this area and deface them and destroy them. That happens a lot more than you may know. People just don't think sometimes and it takes people like you and I to teach them.

This is an old smelter from a mine created in the early 1900s. This smelter has been used, let me tell you. The smelter was built by individual rocks, stacked on top of each other. The inside of it doesn't look like the outside. These individual rocks look like one massive rock inside. In order to melt down minerals like gold, silver, iron, and more, the smelter must reach extremely high temperatures.

Gold has to be around 2000 degrees to start melting. This is a place where the minerals were brought from the mine. Then melted down to not only create bars but to burn the extra material that the miners did not want present. Dirt and mother nature in general will melt away before the precious minerals go down. That being said, the different minerals separate when they become liquid.

This smelter is still intact and I visit it every once in a while to check on it and to examine and compare it to other smelters I find. Luckily for me, it's only about 15 miles from my home.

Remember earlier how I mentioned that you have to keep secrets so people will share information with you and trust you. This is one of those sites.

Author At Spanish Carvings At A Secret Location

I'm free to show my picture, but I will not disclose the location to anyone as I'm still investigating it. I can tell you it's most likely from the mid-1700s, and was carved by the Spanish. It could be a Jesuit secret that still remains unsolved today.

If you look closely, there is a dagger carved by the cross. This is usually a direction indicator telling you to follow the direction the sharp end is pointing too. When I was shown this site, we followed the markers and it took us to another set.

Does this symbol look like a Templar Knights symbol to you? Many think so but in this area, it was used by the Spanish. In this case, it was another symbol to show other Spaniards that they were in the area mining or a treasure was hidden.

The Spanish also used this symbol quite often. It also looks similar to the Templar Knights cross found on the sails of their ships. This photo was taken in a Spanish mine area. I have thousands of photos from hundreds of different sites. I have been involved with many treasures and historical locations. I wish I could share them all with you but that would take so many books to show you.

TWENTY

Treasure Stories And Legends In Every State Of North America

In this chapter, you will find the stories of lost treasures waiting for someone like you to find them. The list was inspired by my research and conversations with people from all over the United States. I hope you find something to grab your interest and passion for treasure hunting.

None of these stories or legends are set in stone. It is up to you to explore and dig up more information before heading out into the field. These are the breadcrumbs leading to your own adventures. Learning about history in your area is extremely important. The hunt is a huge excitement in itself, but the research is worth its own weight in gold. For those of you who are serious about treasure hunting and historical researching, I believe you will find gold in these stories.

The locations in these stories will help you narrow down your hunt and get you started. The dollar amounts attached to these are last reported estimates. Some of them are in the currency of the time, which means they can be worth much, much more today.

Do your homework. Check your state, county, and local laws. Never enter private property without permission. Land grants change all the time and so do the property owners.

And remember to be safe out there. No treasure is worth your life. Treasure hunting and exploring should be fun. The hunt and the history you take in is as valuable in its own way as the hidden riches. Getting outdoors is great for your spirit and mind. Good luck out there and keep an eye out for me—you never know, we might run into each other one day!

The following treasure tales and locations are taken from the notes I've accumulated and kept for many years.

ALABAMA

Railroad Bill Treasure

Morris Slater was a known train robber in the 1890s. His criminal life lasted all of six years. His loot has never been found—none of it. Many believe if you look near the railroads tracks between Atmore and Bay Minette, you might find his cache in a nearby cave.

Lost Gold Of Confederate Coins

The Confederates' cached their accumulated gold and silver by throwing it into a swamp near Athens. The gold and silver coin pieces are believed to have been placed inside two wooden boxes, and to be worth $100,000.

Hickson Treasure

Near Bridgeport, you may find gold coins worth around $30,000 dollars. This treasure today is known as the Hickson Treasure. Some Alabama locals believe they might have the general location narrowed down. This treasure is buried in the ground.

Henry Nunez Hoard

In the 1800s, a man named Henry Nunez operated a ferry. After he died in 1866, rumors of his personal hoard started to spread. It's claimed he buried up to $200,000 dollars in cash, gold, and silver near the ferry landing, which was located on his property. Start your search where Hwy 90 crosses the Perdido River.

The Mcgillivray Plantation Silver

A fur trader named Lachlan McGillivray was known to have buried a cache of silver and coins. The ruins of his home, which was burned down by Indians, can be found four miles North of Wetumpka. If you're lucky enough, you might find the treasure somewhere in or around the ruins. A metal detector would be perfect for this search.

Buzzard Roost Cache

Legends talk about a man named Levi Colbert, who built an inn about three miles west of Cherokee, where he and his family lived for many years. The legend states he buried gold and silver in the woods, west of his home.

Big Sandy Creek Gold

Hardy Clemens was a wealthy politician. He was a slave owner and possessed a farm near Coaling, about 12 miles from Tuscaloosa. Due to the Civil War, he hid and buried $100,000 worth of gold on his property to safeguard it.

ALASKA

The Aleutian Wreck

May 26, 1926, a ship named *Aleutian* struck a pinnacle of hidden rocks under the icy water. Within a matter of seven minutes, the ship sank. Most of the crew abandoned ship, but its cargo of one million American dollars still lies at the bottom of the ocean.

Lake Of The Golden Bar

In 1884, three prospectors crossed the St. Elias Mountains in an area very close to the Yukon River. They found a small lake shining yellow in the sunlight. Upon inspection, the three discovered the shallow sandbank was full of gold nuggets.

Victors Landing Treasure

Surveyors were at the Iskut and Unuk Rivers when one man found a rock, which he put it in his pocket. Later that night, he was inspecting the rock and noticed gold, surrounded by white quartz. The men finished their surveys and left the site. We know that they were at an elevation of 6,400 feet at the time.

The Mad Trapper Johnson Treasure

In 1932, a man known as The Mad Trapper was chased out of the area by several poses, as whenever he was around gunfights occurred. The Mad Trapper was last seen near the Eagle River by the Richardson Mountains. It was reported he may have found an old lost gold mine as evidence pointed to him having a lot of money and gold.

The Yukon Riverboat Columbian

September 25, 1905, a boat named *Yukon Columbian* had a fire onboard. The captain had time to beach the boat along the route to Dawson. The cargo consisted of gold from the mining companies in the area. The sunken boat has never been reported found.

Frank's Gold

Near Dawson, a man named Frank staked a supposedly gold rich gold claim. He was later found frozen in his cabin by his family, but the gold he had reportedly mined was nowhere to be found. Look fifty miles from the Alaskan border and bring your gold detector. Rumors say he buried his processed gold outside by his cabin.

ARIZONA

The Lost Dutchman Mine

Since the 1870s, many have ventured into the Superstition Mountains looking for a rich gold mine. Some say this mine has been worked by the Spanish then rediscovered and worked by a man named Jakob Waltz. While on his deathbed in his home, he gave a map with the location of the mine to a close friend. Although there are claims the mine has been found, my research indicated the true Lost Dutchman Mine is still out there.

Bronco Bill Loses To Wells Fargo

William E. Walters, aka Bronco Bill, was a gunman who successfully robbed a number of trains. Even while imprisoned, he never revealed the location of his hoard of money, gold, and silver. He died in 1921, while repairing a windmill, never recovering his stash. Look near Solomonville and keep your eyes peeled for clues.

Sierra Estrella Buried Gold

Just below Montezuma Head, there's a peak where a man named either Campoy or Ortega (versions of the story vary) hid 3,000 pounds of gold in a cave. He was being chased by local Indians, so he left the gold in the cave before being killed by the Indians. His gold hasn't been recovered.

Canyon Station Treasure Near Kingman

In 1873, a man named McCullum and his partner held up a stagecoach near Canyon Station for $72,000 in gold coins. During the ensuing chase, the posse killed his partner and arrested McCallum. During his trial, McCallum refused to reveal where he buried the coins. McCallum died in prison, but passed on the story to fellow inmates. The coins have never been found.

Flagstaff Outlaw Cache

$125,000 from a stagecoach robbery was hidden in the mountains of Flagstaff. At the outlaws' cabin hideout, located in the surrounding mountains at 8,500 feet, a gun battle ensued between the chasing cavalry and the gang of robbers. All the outlaws were killed and the gold never found. Today's legend says look to the ice caves near the ruins of the cabin. The loot is there somewhere.

Outlaws Steal Outlaw Loot

Davis Peak is an area said to be holding on to several treasures hidden by smugglers from Mexico. Reportedly diamonds, gold statues of the Virgin Mary and Jesus, thirty-nine bars of gold, silver, and more were taken from a bank vault and never recovered. Look for a bald, rounded-granite dome in the mountains, as described by one bandit.

Red Jack Gang

The Red Jack Gang robbed a stagecoach along the Pedro River near Riverside, Arizona. $3,000 of gold was taken. After a posse hunted down the gang, the last bandit standing was found near Wilcox—without the stolen gold.

ARKANSAS

Stuart's Island Buried Cache

A bandit named John Murral supposedly buried two different treasures on an island in the 1800s. If you go to Lake Chicot, near Lake Village, you might be able to find clues.

Brushy Mountains & Jesse James

According to legend, Jessie James helped organize a plan for the KGC to bury thousands of dollars and other treasures in the Brushy Mountains region. Many stagecoaches were robbed to add to the stockpile. Go to the Hot Springs and Plainview area to start your search.

The Twin Springs Treasure

If you like Civil War treasures, go to the outskirts of Wickes in Polk County. Two very large caches of gold bars are said to be in the area. I would engage with the local people and start your search from word of mouth. See where it takes you.

The Madre Vena Treasure

The Madre Vena Treasure is said to be of gold and silver bars and is still lost. Travel to Pineville in the area of Izard County. Do your research and dig up as much information from local archives as you can before you start your search.

Ten Mile House Treasure

There's an old tavern used as the headquarters for Federal troops. On State Route 5, around 9 miles south of Little, you can find the old structure. Many locals say legend tells of small caches around the structure. Bring your metal detector.

CALIFORNIA

Joaquin Murrieta's Stolen Cache

Joaquin Murrieta was a successful miner, but was forced off his claim. He decided to turn to a life of crime. His treasures are said to be many, valuing over $100,000 each. Some believe the treasures are in a hidden cave on Eagle Peak on the south slope of Warner Mountains.

Gunsight Mine Of Death Valley

A silver outcropping was found by the *Lost 49ers* during their delayed travel from Utah to California. Jim Martin took a sample from the outcropping, which he later used as a sight on his gun. He later learned the silver was high in value. Many have looked for the lost outcropping without success.

Hidden Treasure Near Vallecito Station

There's a larger part of the Potrero Canyon known as Treasure Canyon, located just west of Vallecito station and northeast of Descanso. It's said that two hordes of gold coins were buried in the area. Check your local history to learn more about it.

Holden Dick's Stolen Loot

In 1881, a lone bandit robbed a freight wagon of gold in Modoc County. A fight broke out and this bandit went to the western slopes of Warner Mountains. Find where Holden Dick lived and look for a cave. Many people believe that the gold is buried in that cave.

Goose Egg Mine Of El Dorado County

In the area named Goose Neck Ravine, a rich deposit of gold nuggets was discovered by an employed miner. The miner later told his story and showed a nugget he collected. He took others with him, but they couldn't find the exact location again.

Rattlesnake Dick's Stolen Loot

Richard Barter and his gang robbed a Wells Fargo stagecoach in the Trinity Mountains. The gang hid the money, and soon after, the snowfall came. Richard was gunned down, and after that the gang was nowhere to be found. Where's the money? Some diligent research might point you in the right direction…

COLORADO

La Caverna Del Oro: (The Cave Of Gold)

Native Americans tell a story that has been passed down for generations about a treasure of gold hidden deep in a cave at 11,500 feet in elevation on Marble Mountain. Many Spaniards who heard about it lost their lives while searching for it. This story needs some research, but if I lived here, I would look for it.

Arapaho Princess Treasure

The Spanish hid a cache of gold bars near an outcropping they called La Murece (The Doll). The outcropping stands 30 feet tall. Look toward the northwest slope of West Spanish Peak, close to La Verta. You want to look for Spanish treasure, this is the one for you.

Virginia Dale Stage Station

Near Virginia Dale Station, a stagecoach robbery took place and the robbers fled to Long View Hill. The cache is made up of gold coins and legend says it was buried. The bandits were later killed by the cavalry. If you want to look for this treasure, I would do some research and see where it takes you.

Devil's Head Mountain

After staging many attacks and robberies, eight confederate raiders continued their stealing spree, but a violent turn of events stopped the gang from recovering their buried loot. Geneva Gulch is a place to start your search. Find the head of Deer Creek and you'll be close. The bandits hid their treasure wrapped in silk.

The Ten-Cent Treasure

Somewhere between Crawford Ranch and Montrose, many new minted coins are waiting to be found. Dimes to be exact—Denver mints. Along the Gunnison River near the north rim of Black Canyon, treasure hunters found four wagons associated with the story along with some of the coins, but there are still many more to find.

Irish Canyon Silver

Butch Cassidy and the Wild Bunch spent a lot of time in Brown's Park. They had a hideout in the area and supposedly hid $30,000 worth of silver coins in the vicinity. This outlaw cache would be a huge discovery for riches and fame if you do your homework. Look into the local history and reach out to people.

Round Mountain Gold Nuggets

A group of prospectors found a good sized gold nugget at the headwaters of Gunnison River. Unfortunately for them, three of the prospectors were killed by local Ute Indians. The fourth prospector fled to Cochetopa Pass, burying his gold there before the Utes also took his life. There's potentially two treasures—the buried gold and the source of the gold at the headwaters.

CONNECTICUT

Charles Island Treasure

This island has a great story, full of exciting treasures and legends. You need to look into the legends surrounding this island if you live in the area. The first reported date of treasures starts in 1699. Look into the history from then to modern days. A person with a metal detector could do very well here. Make sure you check your state and county treasure hunting laws before getting down to business.

Money Island & Captain Kidd

It's rumored that Captain Kidd buried one of his treasures off Stony Creek. This island is only 12 acres in size, which could make this a somewhat easy target to hunt. Respect the locals and have fun checking into this story. I hope you find something.

Windham Blackbeard's Treasure

Blackbeard is said to have buried some of his treasures in the Windham County area. From a little research, I would suggest investing into a metal detector. Take your time and scout.

DELAWARE

Patty Cannon Treasure

This is linked to the Reserve Underground Railroad and a woman named Patty Cannon. She was a mean person who robbed and killed wealthy men who frequented her tavern. She committed suicide, bud legends say she has over $500,000 of gold buried on what was her land.

Appoquinimink Treasure

Odessa was originally named Appoquinimink back when the town was attacked and burnt down by Indians. Local rumors state that if you go to the old ruins of the town, there are many small treasures that might be found in the vicinity with a metal detector.

Charles Wilson Treasure

Stories claim you could find the millions of dollars is buried in the area. Supposedly, buried chests are filled with precious gems, silver, gold, and more. Look in the Woody Knoll area of Chincoteague island.

Kelley Island Hidden Treasure

Located near Bombay Hook Wildlife Refuge, Captain Kid and James Gillian are said to have both buried treasure on separate occasions.

People have reported finding old coins washing up on the beach. I think there's a few possibilities here. Maybe shipwrecks off the coast as well.

New Castle Mystery

On the west bank of Delaware River, south of Wilmington, pirate stories and treasures fill the area. Some of these tales go back to 1677. Rumor has it a treasure was brought from Madagascar to this location to conceal it. Look for an old well as a starting point.

FLORIDA KEYS

Silver Church Bells

In 1586, a Spanish expedition buried three silver church bells in what's now known as the St. Augustine Park area. The Spanish were keeping the bells from Sir Francis Drake. Not long after, the Spaniards were killed, taking the secret location with them.

Richard Crowe Coins

Richard Crowe died a very wealthy merchant in 1894. After the family reviewed his last recorded will, they found he mentioned burying $60,000 worth of gold coins on his property. Start to look into his history and where his land was located. This could be a good one.

Deleon Springs

If you're a diver, you should look into the DeLeon Springs treasure chest of Ponce de Leon Springs. Some say it's submerged in a nearby cave. Divers have tried. Do you have what it takes? Give it a try.

GEORGIA

Confederate Gold—Chennault Plantation

In 1865, Confederate gold disappeared 100 yards outside of a home. Some say if you look around the Apalachee and Oconee Rivers, the cache containing over $100,000 worth of gold might be found.

Jekyll Island Spanish Treasure

There's not a lot of information about this one, but that could be a positive. Located in Brunswick County, rumors have spread for hundreds of years about Spanish treasure. Not linked to one account, but several possible stories.

St. Simon's Island Silver

Southeast North America is great for Spanish treasures. In Camden County there have been many modern day reports of people finding Spanish silver coins on the beach. Most likely there's a sunken shipwreck in the vicinity. Land and/or water, look for relics.

Tybee Island Coins

This island was a hotspot for pirates. Many stories of buried treasure have come from this area. Some treasure seekers have found old coins along the beach. Go to the mouth of the Savannah River to start your search.

HAWAII

The Burial Chamber Of King Kamehameha:

Some believe Kamehameha, king of Hawaii, was buried in what is now a lost cave. The cave is thought to be in Maui's Lao Valley. Others believe he's buried at the royal palace of Moku'ula in Maui. If you live in this area, talk with locals and try to decipher the clues.

Pirate Treasure Of Oahu's Kaena Point

Six pirate treasure chest of gold and silver a rumored to have been waiting since 1823, for discovery in this area. If you want to start this exploration, head to Kaena Point on the western tip of Oahu island. Search the top of the hill and look for walls of stones.

Lost Tribe Kauai Treasure:

Captain James Cook, a British explorer, was killed by natives in 1779. The King of the natives ordered for his ship to be taken. The treasure found on the ship was thought to be magical and the King ordered it to have it buried on Kauai Island. Look for Waimea Bay, 2 miles Southwest of State Hwy 50.

Peruvian Treasure:

In Honolulu, a cache of riches known as the Peruvian treasure is hidden in the area. I could not find much on this story, but I do believe there's something to search for.

Alfred Devereaux Coins

Over $100,000 dollars of gold and silver coins are said to have been buried by smuggler Alfred Devereaux at Kaho'olawe. After Alfred died, many locals tried to find his treasure, but it has proved elusive.

Captain Cavendish Treasure

A large treasure of $5,000,000 in gold and silver, along with other valuables, was buried by English pirate Captain Cavendish. I've heard Palemano Point is the place to look. I was told this while doing some research with a film producer. His source was from a major network we worked with at the time.

IDAHO

Port Neuf Canyon Stage Robbery

Robbers in 1865, overtook a stagecoach run by the Overland Stage line. A $10,000 reward was offered and posse rode out to find the robbers. The robbers were killed in a shootout with the posse. However, before he died, one of the outlaws gave a brief description, *in the narrow place of Port Neuf Canyon,* as the location where the gang hid their loot.

City Of Rocks Buried Treasure

Local legends say many treasures are buried close to the City of National Reserve. One cache, known as the Jim Lonney treasure, is supposedly full of gold bullion—over $100,000 worth. Start your search at Almo Cache Peak.

Camas Creek Gold

More research needs to be done, but somewhere in a one-mile radius around Camas, there's said to be a treasure worth $25,000 in gold buried on the banks of Camas Creek.

Mccammon Millions Of Gold Treasure

Three hundred pounds of gold was stolen during a stage coach robbery. This treasure would be worth around $6,000,000 today. It's buried somewhere close to McCammon at a place called Robbers Roost, supposedly about three-quarters of a mile north of McCammon.

Priest Lake Treasure Of Gold

At Priest Lake, a prospector named Zak Stoneman's mules died after eating poisonous weeds. He had no choice but to bury his gold. Look north of Priest River and three-quarters of a mile below Priest Lake. Zak came back for his gold at a later time but he was unsuccessful in recovering it.

Cassia County Treasure

Sheepherders and cattlemen became involved in a small range war. During the conflict, both sides stayed in the area of Cassia where they buried small treasures so the other side would not prosper from the riches. Look for Deep Creek and Shoshone Creek to start your search.

Robbers Gulch Gold Cache

Stagecoach bandits had a hideout on the Salmon River, around five miles southwest of White Bird. A stagecoach robbery gave the bandits a take of $75,000 in gold. The treasure has never been recovered. Many locals believe the gold is near the outlaw's hideout.

Rogerson Outlaw Robbery

In 1888, an outlaw robbed the Jarbidge-Idaho stagecoach. His attempt to get away was unsuccessful as he was killed by a posse. However, the gold was never found, and many think he buried it fifteen miles west of Rogerson. Look on the east side of Browns Bench.

ILLINOIS

Mysterious Hurricane Creek

This area has an ancient legend of giant skeletons discovered. Natives called this a sacred site and protected it from white settlers. The natives spoke of many ancient treasures belonging to the ancient burial site and its people. Start your search at Hurricane Creek.

Lost Stash Of Henri De Tonti

Henri de Tonti was a powerful person in Illinois between 1685 and 1702. Rumors have lingered for many years about a $100,000 in gold that he buried around Starved Rock. Henri told a priest about the gold before he died. That's how this story has been kept alive.

James Gregory Stash

James Gregory was a successful, wealthy man but he didn't trust banks. He didn't even trust his wife. Neighbors in Marion County, around his property, would say that they sometimes found him sneaking and ducking around on his property. After James died, his wife looked on the property and didn't find his stash. Find his old property boundaries and see where that takes you.

The Sweetin Home Ghost

In 1848, a mansion was built by Azarsh Sweetin. During the Civil War, he buried jars of gold coins on his property. Later he had an accident and lost his memory and so couldn't remember where the gold was placed. The mansion ruins have been picked apart, but the property has not yet given up its secrets.

INDIANA

Josiah Hite Coins

Josiah Hite was a counterfeiter who lived in Charlestown. During the 1800s, he was arrested but escaped. He never returned to the area and his cache of coins remained where he hid them in Charlestown.

Gangster Jim Genna Cash

Known gangster, Jim Genna, buried a large amount of cash in a steel box. The FBI arrested Genna, but even after Genna told them the location of the hidden cash, they couldn't find it. Inspect the area of route 6 and near 331 by Bremen.

Wabash River Money Stash

Along the banks of the Wabash River, there's supposed to be a large amount of money hidden. If you would like to look for this treasure, look between Geneva and Berne.

The Reno Brothers Treasure

Hidden under an old foundation, you may be able to track down $96,000 of gold and cash. The Reno Brothers robbed a train in 1868 in Jackson County. Unfortunately, the exact location was lost when the brothers died.

IOWA

Fort Atkinson's Lost Payroll

Fort Atkinson was attacked in 1848 by Indians. Out of fear, an officer buried the payroll very close to the fort—$7,000 worth in gold. Search near Decorah in Winneshiek to find the remains of the fort. It can't be too far away from there.

A Merchant's Gold At The Nishnabotna River

Do your research on this story to get more information. A stash of $75,000 of gold was buried along the Nishnabotna River. There's not much to report or more information, but in this case, that could be good. Be an investigator and maybe you'll hit the motherlode.

Red Brussels' Cache

Red gained his wealth by stealing horses and reselling them. He was eventually hung. The town's people believed he buried $40,000 of gold coins on the Mississippi River, a few miles to the North of Sabula.

Miners Creek Payroll

This contains info of two Army payrolls along Miners Creek. Go to Guttenberg, and follow Miners Creek with an open eye. Look for any clues. There has to be something that stands out to help you find these payrolls. A metal box may have been used to bury the treasures so using a detector is advisable.

Thomas Nelson's Gold

Thomas Nelson was a soldier. Due to fear of his neighbors at Wheeler Ranch, he told a story of digging a three-foot hole and burying his gold along the Winnebago River near Horseshoe Bend.

KANSAS

Fort Dodge Silver

Jesus Martinez was travelling with a wagon train when it was attacked by Indians. When the battle was over, Jesus found twenty-one bags, each containing $1,000 of silver coins, totaling $21,000 in value. He was able to make off with the silver and buried it somewhere near Fort Dodge on Hwy 400, east of Dodge City.

Hamilton County Stage Station

Felix Goldman knew he was being tracked for three days by outlaws. Scared of losing his gold and silver, he buried $17,000. A few days later, he was reported dead. Hamilton County and the southwest portion, near the Colorado border, is where you should start to look.

Fleagle Gang Buried Cache

The famous Fleagle Gang robbed a bank in 1928, and made off with $100,000 in gold, silver, and cash. It is reputed that they buried it either at Battle Canyon or in Chicken Ranch, which is close to Branson.

Pawnee Rock

A wagon train was attacked by Indians. The survivors said they buried their valuables in the Buffalo Wallows area. Winter came and went, but the survivors didn't come back.

KENTUCKY

Sandy River Silver Bars

In the 1760s, Jonathan Swift buried a huge amount of silver and silver ore along the breaks of the Sandy River. Legend says he found a cave and the silver remains there today. He traveled along Hwy 80 near Elkhorn City by the Pine Mountain.

Moore's Treasure

In the 1880s, Moore hid a coin hoard on his property. After some trouble with his hired hands, he was killed. His murderers were unsuccessful in their search for his hoard. The hired hands went to prison for Moore's murder where they talked about the story of Moore's hidden stash.

Military Money, Pokes Loot

From 1861 to 1862, Confederate troops stayed at Camp Beauregard southwest of Mayfield. Many stories have been told about the troops burying small caches of their own valuables at their camp. Find the camp and take your metal detector to uncover relics and artifacts.

James Langstaff Gold Coins

James owned quite a bit of land before his death and he was wealthy. James left his wife a letter before he died, telling her that he buried $20,000 of gold coins at either South Third Street or Broadway in Paducah. In the letter, he mentioned a tree marker by a cottonwood.

LOUISIANA

Fortune Of Gabriel Fuselier De La Claire

De la Claire was a French aristocrat who arrived in Louisiana in 1748. His grandson buried his fortune at the plantation home during the Civil War. During the war, the home was burnt to the ground. The $500,000 buried treasure was never found. The home was built in Grand Coteau.

Monsieur Richarde Of Shreveport

Monsieur Richarde buried his wealth in his garden around the beginning of the 1900s. This treasure wasn't recovered by him for unknown reasons. His home was around the Cobar Farm and the vicinity of Riverboat Captain Joseph Boisseau.

Limerick Plantation Mystery

I'm hoping you can find more about this story. It's hard when I'm in the western states. Near Monroe, a treasure was buried at the old Limerick Plantation property. People involved are unknown, but information may be discovered in local library archives.

Old Camp Place Treasures

Many legends of treasures have come from the area of Old Camp Place. Civil War refugees played a big part. Find the history of these stories and you will find the location.

MAINE

Starboards Creek—Brothers Island Treasures

The Brothers Island is well known for treasures, especially pirate loot. Captain Harry Thompson hid treasures by marking trees with symbols. These symbols act as clues to point the way to riches. Modern and old searches have been conducted with nothing discovered.

Damaris Cove Island—Pirate Treasures

Dixie Bull was a famous pirate known to travel to many islands around Damaris Cove. His treasures have been widely rumored and speculated about, but nothing has been brought to the public about a discovery. Many believe the treasures are still actually buried on Damaris Cove.

Jewell Island And Captain Kidd

Captain Kidd was known to have a great hiding spot on Jewell Island. In fact, there have been several discoveries, but many believe they were just the tip of the iceberg. If you ask me, I would explore the area and learn more about these discoveries. It may land you some booty.

Machias River And Black Sam Bellamy

This is a story backed by credibility and history. Black Sam Bellamy built a large log house close to the main part of Machias River. After years of stealing this was the place where he and his gang hid their riches. The treasures are said to have grown so large, Sam decided to quit the life of a pirate, but not before he carried out one last ship robbery, from which he never returned.

Penobscot Bay—Place Of Hidden Riches

Penobscot River is a resting place for many sunken ships and their cargo. This is also known as a pirate's loot area as well. Some famous pirates are said to have buried their riches near Isle Au Haut and Hog Island.

MARYLAND

The Mansion House Treasure

Northwest of Baltimore, a farm holds a large secret of a large treasure cache. It's said that a treasure of $65,000 was buried on the property, belonging to a very expensive and large mansion. Find the location of the mansion, and you may be able to find the treasure.

Jacques Champlain Coins

Jacques Champlain was said to have buried a large treasure of $150,000 in gold coins. He was a successful merchant during his time. There's land that belongs to a farm near Catonsville. This is where the "X" is marked on the map.

Jake Hole Treasure

On the south shore of the Chaptank River, near Lodgecliffe, you may find a treasure hidden by Jack Hole, a pirate who visited the area. It's rumored he buried one of his treasures worth $200,000 there. This could be worth millions today.

MASSACHUSETTS

Sunken Treasure Of The Whydah

There is still treasure to be found from Whydah Gally and his pirate ship. Modern day discoveries have revealed many artifacts and the shipwreck itself. A new report has recently surfaced documenting $400,000 of gold coins stolen right before his ship sank in only fourteen feet in water, about five hundred feet off the shore of Wellfleet. The coins have not been found.

Short Beach And Grover's Cliff

Both Spanish and British coins have been found on the beaches of Short Beach and Grover's Cliff. These coins can be worth thousands of dollars each. After some research, I'm guessing there's some shipwrecks just off the coast. Diving and metal detecting may yield good results here.

Mysterious Blue Rock Found

A farmer named James Roland Cooke heard pirates on the shore near where he lived in 1824. He waited for them to leave and then discovered a blue rock was placed where the pirates were digging. After hunting for the law, he brought them back to the spot, only he couldn't find it. No recorded discoveries have been made in this area of Chappaquiddick Island, near Cape Poge.

Money Bluff Buried Treasure

This area has many stories of hidden pirate loot. Deer Island near Money Bluff is the area to start your search. A few tried to locate the treasure in 1824, but they were unsuccessful. Bring a metal detector.

Hessian Loot In Dalton

During the Revolutionary War, the British traveled to Dalton and found themselves outnumbered. Due to fear of losing their valuables, they buried their treasure in a short cannon barrel and placed it in the woods. The townspeople knew the British had buried something of value, but were unable to find it.

MICHIGAN

High Island Lost Treasure

Northern Lake Michigan has a long history of early visits by the Spanish, French, and early Mormon settlers. About 10 miles west of Beaver Island, west of the Straits of Mackinac, is the place to start your search. A treasure hunter reported finding Spanish silver coins in that area, so it's possible there are more waiting to be discovered.

The Henry Dansman Treasure

If you're looking for an interesting adventure, somewhere between Lake August and Village of Posen, on county route 65, rumors have it that a wealthy farmer named Henry Dansman buried a cache of diamonds, gold, and silver coins on his property.

Cat Head Point Loot

In the aftermath of the destruction caused by the Great Chicago Fire of 1871, banks were looted and the ill-gotten gains allegedly buried nearby. Start your search near Northpoint on county route 201. I would suggest listening to what locals have to say and bring a metal detector.

Drummond Island

At Lake Huron, on the southwest end of the island, a British Commander left a treasure. His name was General Monk, and he buried a large iron chest that belonged to the British Army near where the old fort once stood. Find the ruins of the fort and start searching there.

MINNESOTA

Minnesota Old Soldiers Home

Somewhere at or around the location of the Minnesota Old Soldiers Home, you might be able to track down a mystery. A man supposedly buried $5,000 in gold coins. When he returned, he couldn't find the location of his riches.

Ma Barker And The Alvin Karpis Gang

The Alvin Karpis Gang and Ma Barker succeeded in their demand for a $200,000 ransom. They buried the money—paid in five and ten dollar bills—in a metal box under a fence post. It was never recovered. This would be a large box. Look around along Hwy 52 between Chatfield and Rochester.

Thomas Fontaine Cash

There's not a lot of info on this story, but that doesn't mean it's not true. Legend has it a large amount of money was buried on a farm once owned by Thomas Fontaine. This is a quiet story, so if there's something there you may have a good chance of finding it.

Old Sherburne Gold Coins

Somewhere near the Blue Hill township, a hermit named Old Sherburne was a known penny pincher. When he died in 1882, his brother searched for Old Sherburne's money—rumored to be in gold worth $40,000—which was supposedly buried near the Blue Hill glacial deposit mound. He didn't find it, but maybe you will.

The Lost Payroll Of The Civil War

I would look for this treasure in Baldwin County, near Elk Lake. Soldiers buried two saddle bags of gold coins under an oak tree. Local Indians stopped their chase, thinking the soldiers were dead. The soldiers came out of hiding, but before they could recover their loot, a fire broke out and the area was destroyed. The soldiers never found their cache, which is rumored to be still there.

MISSISSIPPI

The Buried Treasure Of Chief Toby Tubby

Chief Toby was buried in the traditional tomb of the local natives. They buried him with his riches of gold in an unknown location. Family members heard of his death and were unsuccessful in locating the burial site. This story has a lot of information. I would do your research online to get an approximate location and then go from there.

The Gore Buried Fortune

This is perfect for you metal detectorist. T.P. Gore made millions in his lifetime. He buried around $400,000 in gold coins very close to his home. Look to Calhoun City to start your research. He was a known man so documents of his property should be in archival records. Locate where his home was built and go from there.

The Buried Treasure Of Pirate Patrick Scott

Patrick Scott was considered a small-time pirate, but was actually simply a pest. He would steal from ships, taking anything of value such as guns, coins, gold, silver. He was a slippery thief who was able to evade the law. It's said he buried treasures around Ocean Springs in Jackson County. He was finally caught and later died in prison in 1844. His treasure troves have not been recovered.

The Pirate House Underground Tunnels

The famous pirate named Jean Laffite had a very large crew of thieving men. His house had secret tunnels underneath it where his stolen treasures were placed. The Pirate House was destroyed by hurricane Camille, but many have searched for the underground tunnels. The house was located at the Bay of St. Louis.

MISSOURI

Alf Bolin's Outlaw Loot

One of Alf Bolin's gang members came looking for the treasure of buried gold and silver. He told local people he heard firsthand about the clues. He looked for a cave in the Fox Creek area. According to some maps, it's in the area of Section 20, Township 22, Range 20. Check your local mining records. This should get you pointed in the right direction.

Legend Of Bone Hill

By Bone Hill Graveyard near Levasy, there are the ruins of stone walls. As slave labor was building those walls some treasures were found. The previous owner is unknown, but someone must have been hiding their loot here. Many locals still believe that treasures can be found in the vicinity due to legends and evidence.

Lost Copper Mine In The Ozark Hills

In Current River, near Jacks Fork, there's a rich copper mine that was discovered and worked by Joseph Slater. Townspeople witnessed him selling large amounts of copper. He did stake a claim to the location of the mine, but nobody has been able to locate it. Look for the old mining paperwork. The mine is located somewhere in the Ozark Hills.

Parson Keithly's Hidden Gold

Parson Keithly has some history as an odd individual who preached on Sunday and then disappeared for days afterwards. He was a prospector in California and brought some gold back home. He would often visit a cave near to his home, and surviving family members believe he buried his gold there.

MONTANA

Treasure At Little Bighorn

There's many legends about Little Bighorn, but I know from my research there's more than just the battle. I've not been able to go hunt for myself, but throughout the years, I've heard many theories of buried war treasures, and of conspiracies and cover-ups in the area.

The Henry Plummer Gang Buried Treasure

Sheriff turned outlaw leader Henry Plummer had a hideout with his gang at Rattlesnake Ranch. Plummer was ruthless committing murders and robberies with abandon. Theories abound about hidden loot near the gang's hideout. A metal detector and a keen eye may be all you need to find something.

Chinese Grade Murdered Miner

The booming mining town of Beartown was located on the Clear Fork River between Drummond and Bearmouth. An outlaw group called the Beartown Roughs robbed many of the local miners. One story states a Chinese miner was robbed by outlaws who then buried five pounds of gold (worth $140,000 today) close to a mine in the area.

Hollow Top Mountain Cave Of Gold

The Plummer Gang strikes again! In the mid-1860s, the gang buried a gold treasure worth around $800,000 seven miles northeast of Waterloo city. Look for a cave is what the legend says. Scout the area for a cave opening and you may strike it rich.

NEBRASKA

David Colbert Mccanles' Lost Fortune

David McCanles was killed by Wild Bill Hickok in 1861. Prior to his demise, David built a bridge for the Oregon Trail and made a fortune. It's said he buried $75,000 of gold coins in an iron box, near the Rock Creek Station.

The Treasure At Lodgepole Creek

In 1867, a treasure worth $720,000 (modern day value) was buried along Lodgepole Creek. The outlaws who robbed the stagecoach were shortly surrounded by a large posse. The outlaws buried the gold in a hurry and escaped. The outlaws came back for the gold at a later time, but were unable to find it again due the rush they were in when they buried it.

Buffalo Bill's Secret Stash

Buffalo Bill has many stories and this one might suit you well. Supposedly, Bill buried $17,000 worth of gold coins somewhere on the grounds of Scout's Rest Ranch. Locate the property and you may be in luck.

NEVADA

Tim Cody's Lost Ledge

Tim Cody was a prospector who created a basecamp by Stewart Springs about fifteen miles from Goldyke. While looking for minerals, Cody found a cave which led out to a ledge from which he noticed a quartz view. He needed to go back to base camp, but when he returned he was unable to locate the cave and the ledge again.

Lost Whiskey, Wagon Loa

In 1880, a man hauling a wagonload of whiskey was caught in a storm, during which his horse got loose and ran off. Abandoning his wagon, he proceeded on foot until he came to a ranch in Oasis Valley. When he returned to where he thought he'd left his wagon, it was gone along with its contents. He thought that the high winds covered the wagon with the sand in the area. Anyone thirsty?

Gold Coins In The Genoa Hills

On his death bed, a miner confessed to robbing a payroll pouch. He claimed he buried $20,000 dollars of gold coins under a pine tree close to where the robbery took place near Genoa. He admitted he never went back for it.

The Lost Breyfogle Gold

Inn 1863, a prospector named Charles Breyfogle founded the Breyfogle. The story goes, he was wandering the desert around the Amargosa River Valley. After days of walking, he found quartz flecked with gold. I've heard of this story many times.

Spanish Massacre Site

In the Mormon Peak area of Mesquite, I have found evidence on a natives' panel explaining a battle with the Spanish. The Spanish were killed and buried in the vicinity. In the case of many of the massacre sites I've researched, if natives were involved, they usually buried the Spanish bodies and belongings on the battleground. Start your search near Moapa Peak.

NEW HAMPSHIRE

Wentworth By The Sea

In 1775, Governor Wentworth buried gold and silver coins to keep them safe during the Revolutionary War. The coins were in a metal box and placed somewhere between Portsmouth and Smithtown in a heavily wooded area. Great prospects for detectorists with the time to scout the area thoroughly.

Blackbeard's Isles Of Shoals

Blackbeard and his pirates reportedly visited a small town tavern on the island. Supposedly, Blackbeard buried some treasures while he was there, drinking and socializing with his crew. Check for permission from the landowner before hunting.

Sandy Gordon White Island

Sandy Gordon was a captain of a pirate group for a few years. There's not a lot I know about this other than people have told me that somewhere on White Island around 1716, Gordon and his crew buried a treasure for safekeeping.

John Quelch's Treasure Of Gold

In the 1600's, pirate John Quelch buried a large treasure on an island. This treasure is thought to be nine pounds of gold and a hundred and ninety pounds of silver. Some say he buried it on the west side of Appledore Island, while others say it was Star Island. This is a big treasure.

NEW JERSEY

John Bacon's Long Beach Loot

Several ship treasures were acquired by Captain John Bacon, who was loyal to the British during the Revolutionary War. On Oct. 25, 1782, his crew took many of these treasures and buried them on the Isles of Shoals. Start your search close to the Lighthouse of Barnegat.

Aaron Kitchell's Fortune In Hanover

Aaron Kitchell worked for the Senate in the late 1700s. He was also a friend of George Washington. Aaron left U.S. minted gold coins with his wife to keep safe. Unfortunately, she subsequently died while he was away on travel without letting him know what she did with the coins, which have never been found. Legends say she buried them somewhere in Hanover.

The Lost Fortune Of The Pine Barrens Bandit

It's said the Fagan Gang created underground hideouts in the Farmingdale area. Many locals believe loot from their robberies were hidden there. The Fagan gang were either shot or hung and never revealed the location of their hideouts. Find their hideouts and you'll likely find their treasure.

NEW MEXICO

Army Payroll In San Juan County

In 1874, Samuel Wharton and Thomas Horton robbed a stagecoach. They traveled north with the $50,000 of gold coins. The cavalry was hot on their trail and they buried the coins by a rock shaped like an arch. The two men were captured and imprisoned. They talked to others about the location of the stash, but it was never found.

Victorio Peak Mystery Treasure

On Victorio Peak, the treasure of San Andres is said to be hidden. There are many documents that allude to the treasure. If I lived in the area, I would do some research and then head to the area and look for clues.

The Lost Padre Mine

An old Spaniard on his deathbed told a priest named LaRue that he had seen and been involved with Padre Mine. Rich gold deposits were said to be in the mine, which was in the mountains around El Paso. The Spaniard claimed the mine was a day's ride north of El Paso near three small peaks. Look for a small spring and a path leading to the east near the most visible peak.

Rockhounding In The Prineville Region

If you like rock hounding, the Prineville area is a good place to go. All kinds of different rocks and crystal formations have been found in New Mexico. Do some searches online and track down the best areas. This proves to be a great family and friend activity.

NEW YORK

Butlersbury Mansion Caches

There was a mansion built near Fonda by Switzer Hill. In 1742, the owners John and William Butler robbed many patriots during the Revolutionary War. Legend says, they buried several caches of stolen loot on their property.

Grand Island Treasures

Clairieux was a French merchant and legends say he buried many treasures in the 1700s, between Buffalo and Niagara Falls, close to the Niagara River. Clairieux owned a store and home and that's where it is thought he buried his valuables.

Money Ponds At Montauk Point

On Long Island, Captain Kidd was said to bury a treasure large enough for a king. Some say the treasure was spread out on the islands like Setauket & Oyster Bay. Many people have told me to find the Montauk lighthouse and start looking there for clues.

NORTH CAROLINA

The Gander Hall Plantation Silver & Gold

Legend has it there's a plantation home about 2 miles west of Wilmington. Locals have mentioned that $30,000 dollars of gold and silver coins were buried near the home during the war due to fear of it being found and taken. Find the plantation and start your search.

Anne Blyth Coins

Anne Blyth was a known female pirate of her time who hid many treasures. Stories say she buried silver and gold coins near Fort Caswell. Go to the mouth of the Cape Fear River, heading south of the Southport region.

Shackleford Banks Civil War Silver

During the Civil War, a Confederate ship was attacked by a Union gunship. The Confederate ship was driven ashore at Shackleford Banks. The crew saved a treasure of silver coins and buried it along the high sand dunes. The Confederate were killed and the treasure is still missing. On the southwest side of Harker's Island is where to start searching.

NORTH DAKOTA

The Robbed Payroll

A Civil War paymaster was robbed and a large cache of gold coins were taken by the outlaws. The outlaws were soon tracked to an area near Sunset Butte, which is close to the town of Bowman. The payroll was never discovered. You might have the drive to find it.

The Lost Detachment Gold

This is also known as the Lost Soldiers' Cache. The treasure involves U.S. troops and $3,000 of gold dust. General George Crook and his men patrolled the area of the Black Hills during the gold rush. They reported a miner who buried his gold and they kept an eye out for outlaws trying to find and steal it.

Dr. Dibbs Lost Mine Reports

Dr. William Dibbs has written statements of finding mine shafts and tunnels near Deep Creek in Bowman County. Because of these reports, I would go to the known area and do some hiking and exploring. Old gold mines present not only minerals but also open doors to finding relics and artifacts left behind from the era. Keep an eye out for anything that sticks out.

OHIO

Turkeyfoot Creek Treasure

There's a legend from local natives that mentions a buried treasure. The natives say gold was buried on the inside bend of Turkeyfoot

Creek. From there, you'll want a good metal detector to scout the creek. This could be a group activity event.

Lost French Gold Of Minerva

Local Indians reported to the French that British troops were coming to attack them. The French loaded their pack horses with two thousand pounds of gold and headed for Fort Laurens. The British attacked the fort as well and the French fled, but not before burying the treasure where the three rivers fork, leaving a symbol carved in a tree to mark its location.

John Dillinger's Loot

Here's a good gangster treasure for you. In Jackson County, John Dillinger buried a treasure of $825,000 on a farm owned by a man named Bailey. Dillinger must have had a connection with Bailey, and the home is said to be about eleven miles outside of town.

Gold Bars At Fairport Harbor

There's a legend of a treasure worth $100,000, two miles from Lake Erie. In 1862, a bank robber buried the gold bars three feet deep and thirty paces northeast of a large oak tree on the river bed. From Lake Erie, near Fairport Harbor, off the Grand River you may find the oak tree.

Fat Nicholas Of Hispaniola Treasure

The pirate named Nicholas D. LePetomaine, aka Fat Nicholas, buried a good sized treasure. Many locals believe the area to look is in Eden Park. If you want to look for clues, you're good but if you want to metal detect, check into permits and local laws.

OKLAHOMA

Battle Of Kansas Gold

When the Civil War broke out two federal wagons from the Confederates carrying gold coins were travelling through Kansas. Outlaws attacked the wagons and robbed them. The outlaws hid the gold in a cave said to be close to the Blue River. More killings happened and the gold was not found.

Arbuckle Stolen Payroll

If you can find a cave near Mill Creek, you might be in luck. Go to the Arbuckle Mountains and find a cave opening. Legend says a stolen Army payroll consisting of gold and silver coins was hidden in the cave.

Old Fort Sill Trading Post Well

You need to track down the location of old Fort Sill. In 1892, a treasure of $100,000 in gold and silver coins was hidden at the bottom of an old well. Locals say the well is now covered by land and vegetation. Check old records for the fort. Look for anything that might point to the location of this well.

Samuel Stewart's Gold

If you have a metal detector this is a story for you. In 1933, Samuel Stewart buried $5,000 in gold coins on Gyp Hill. It's said that the coins were $20 pieces of gold and buried in a large metal box—potentially easy pickings with a good detector, patience, and diligence.

Sugarloaf Mountain Treasure

$2,000,000 worth of gold bars are said to be buried not far from Boise City. Ten miles from Boise, to the northwest, you'll find Sugarloaf Peak. A French miner buried it and told others the story many years later. He mentioned that he never came back for it.

OREGON

Buried Treasure Of Neahkahnie Mountain

Due to Spanish history not much has been recorded, but I've worked many Spanish stories with less info. In the 1600s, Spanish explorers buried treasures at the foot of Neahkahnie Mountains. It's said by locals that it's either on the slopes or at the foot of the mountain.

Skeleton Mountain Payroll

There's a $60,000 treasure of payroll gold coins about twenty miles east of Glendale on Skeleton Mountain. The outlaw who stole the gold coins confessed his crimes when he was arrested, but only gave a vague location as to the where the stash was hidden.

Sexton Mountain Pass Gold

In the 1850s, local Indians chased down some outlaws and killed them. They then discovered gold bars among the dead bodies. The Indians claim they tossed the gold in a gully on the Rouge River, ten miles northwest of Grants.

The Silent Paymaster Of Fort Grant

A Fort Grant paymaster was kept very busy trading money for gold, silver, gold dust, and other valuables. The paymaster would sometimes put some of his treasure in a large iron kettle and bury it in a secret place. I believe if you can locate the fort, you can use a metal detector to scan the area and come up with some nice finds.

PENNSYLVANIA

The Lost Silver Cave

A settler in the late 1700s found a cave and took shelter inside. While he spent time in there, he discovered the cave held a secret—virgin silver veins ran throughout the parts he explored. History tells of many local Indians using virgin silver to trade for goods. This suggests the story may be true and the Indians knew where the cave was.

American Robin Hood

David Lewis was known for his life of crime. He stole from the rich and he gave to the poor. During his time in prison, he wrote a memoir before dying. It states he hid $10,000 of riches in a small cave by Juniata River, and $20,000 along Conodoguinet Creek. Find that memoir and you may find the treasure.

The Union Soldiers' Stash

U.S. troops' wagons were carrying several dozen gold bars to Washington. Due to being accosted by Confederate troops, the gold was hidden somewhere on the Susquehanna River by Harrisburg. One party turned to the Lock Haven area. Reports say dead mules and horse were found from the U.S. troops but not the gold. Nothing has been said about the gold ever being recovered.

Frontenac's Fortune

Canadian explorers were carrying kegs full of gold coins worth $350,000. After trouble with natives, they buried their treasure for safekeeping. Two of the Canadians were priests and claim they carved a cross into a large stone to mark the treasure's location. It's said that the treasure has remained in Potter County to this day.

RHODE ISLAND

Pirate Charles Harris Newport Cliffs

Check your local legends and history, but pirate Charles Harris is said to have buried a treasure in the area. Many believe the treasure chest is at Newport Beach, Newport Cliffs, Rhode Island.

The Prescott Farm Coins

A farm was built in 1710 by the Overings family, one of the richest in New England. General Richard Prescott also lived there. Legends say the General buried a large amount of gold coins on the farm. Locate the farm on route 144 in Portsmouth to begin your search.

Hog Island Treasures

Little has been told and recorded about this, but some legends speak of Captain William Kidd coming to Hog Island to bury his treasures. There may be several treasures to find if someone takes the time to investigate.

SOUTH CAROLINA

Williamson Plantation Treasure

Apparently, Captain Huck and his men accumulated a huge amount of treasure in their time, some of which is supposedly buried around the property of the Williamson Plantation. The plantation buildings are long gone, but the buried treasures are said to remain. Use local library archives to search for clues.

The Legend Of Captain Jack Murrell

Some Spanish gold and silver coins have been found in the area, but this is about Captain Jack Murrell's buried treasure. Thirteen miles south of Myrtle Beach, Jack and his men buried stolen treasures from ships in a marshy area. Grab your detector and start searching along the shores.

Lost British Payroll Treasure

Lying at the bottom of the Great Pee Dee River could be a British treasure waiting for you. A British barge ship full of supplies overturned and sank in the river. Legend says it had a large payroll cargo onboard.

North Island British Looting

In 1781, many plantations were looted by the British. It's said that the British used North Island at the mouth of Winyah Bay as their headquarters. The British headquarters was overtaken and the British were all killed. The treasures looted from homes in the area were not discovered at the time, and many locals believe the treasures are still there waiting to be found.

Indian Treasure At Mulberry Plantation

Legend says that during the Yamasee War, the plantation was used to fight Indian renegades. Later, many of the Indians were caught and hanged. It's also believed someone buried a huge treasure of jewelry, gold, and silver on the property of the plantation to keep it safe. Visit the 800 acres on the Copper River between Moncks Corner and Charleston in Berkeley County.

SOUTH DAKOTA

Cuthbert Ducharme Gold

In Sheridan there's a tract of land known as Burnt Ranch. A soldier murdered a miner for his gold, and the gold was then buried by the soldier. The miner was named Norway McCully, and his lost gold was never recovered. Some say to look in the O Valley location.

The Bear Mountain Gold

In 1879, two miners named Humphrey and Shafer struck it rich. They had so much gold, they buried $1,000,000 worth. Word spread of the fortune and outlaws came calling. The two miners were captured by the bandits, but would not give up the hidden location. The miners were killed and the secret supposedly still lies on the west side of Bear Mountain in Pennington County.

Gray Foot's Loot

A bank loot of $56,000 was robbed by an unknown Indian in 1862. He got away with a large sack full of coins. Many people think he hid it somewhere along the eastern shores of Long Lake.

TENNESSEE

Little Dover Confederate Treasure

There's a Confederate gold and silver treasure hidden at Little Dover. During the Civil War, a cache of gold and silver was placed here for safe keeping. Legend says the original owner never came back for it.

Monteagle Civil War Treasures

There's a cave on Monteagle Mountain that holds a Civil War treasure. It's said Union troops buried a large treasure in a cave on the mountain. Look for a cave opening. Explore and hike around to discover potential clues.

Lost Delosie Mine

Right on the border of North Carolina and Tennessee is where the Delosie Mine is said to be lost. Because of this mine, and others like it in the area, many people believe there are many treasures waiting to be found, including artifacts, ruins, gold, and silver.

Dollar Hill Payroll Chest

The U.S. Army is said to have buried a $15,000 gold coin treasure on Dollar Hill. Go outside of the city to start your search. All I know is the gold belongs to a payroll. Search the outer boundaries of Clarksburg.

Jb Moore Loot

Near Lexington an outlaw named JB Moore and his two sons were killed attempting to rob a stagecoach. Legend says the stolen loot from previous robberies was never found, but buried somewhere about five miles north of Natchez Trace Park.

TEXAS

The Lost Bill Kelley Mine

Locals say the Bill Kelley mine is located in the harsh Big Bend County. Legend says this is a cursed mine, but one of the richest in all of America. On the Mexican side of the Rio Grande is where the lost mine was supposedly discovered abandoned. This is a great story with a lot of information now on the internet.

Red River Treasure

In 1892, Lewis Franklin was appointed the first Marshal in the area. When outlaws robbed the First National Bank in Bowie, Lewis caught up to them by the river at Rock Crossing. The outlaws were captured and 18,000 paper bills were recovered, but not the $10,000 in gold dollars. The Outlaws were later hanged, meaning the gold is still out there ready to be found.

Singer Treasure On Padre Island

John Singer and his family were shipwrecked on Padre Island. They decided to buy a large amount of land on the island. Later, he sided with the Union and was chased off by Confederates. Before leaving, he buried $80,000 on his ranch. Storms hit and he was unable find the treasure again. Modern day treasure hunters are looking, but no one has found it yet—it's still up for grabs.

Spider Rock Treasure

I don't know too much about this legend, but I thought you may be able to find more information and possibly make a discovery. Somewhere in West Texas, a lost treasure belonging to the Spanish is said to lay hidden. Many reported finding marks on rock and more Spanish clues.

UTAH

Castle Gate Lost Treasure

I have personally looked for this treasure. My team and I debuted on the Travel Channel show called *The Legend Of... With Chris Jericho*. The treasure is rumored to be hidden by Robber's Roost. All that's left of the hideout is a chimney. There are many slot canyons near there and it would be easy to hide something. Be on the lookout for any clues.

Montezuma's Treasure

The Aztecs possibly lived in the Utah area before they moved to Mexico. Some say the Aztecs brought their treasure back when Cortes stormed their capitol in 1521. Many treasure hunters have looked for the treasure around Kanab. Many ancient artifacts and even carved symbols have been found. Johnson Canyon is the hotspot. Beware of the landowners.

Lost Josephine Mine

The Josephine Mine is said to be one of the most famous Spanish mines in the world. Some local treasure hunters believe it is atop Hoyt Peak, near Kamas. Others believe the mine is in the Henry Mountains. A found Spanish waybill states that many gold and silver bars (worth $5,000,000) were stored behind a wooden door inside the mine with a chain and lock.

Spanish Treasure Of The Henry Mountains

Tales of many Spanish treasures and even mines surround this area. It's a very remote mountain and only a few old timers know the legends well. For over a hundred years, explorers have found numerous different Spanish artifacts. The mystery is far from being solved. I would work with someone in the area who knows the mountain well.

The Lost Rhoades Mines

The Rhoades Mines are probably the most famous stories ever told in Utah. Thomas Rhoades was shown a few rich gold and silver Spanish mines by the Ute Indians. He promised only to use the riches for the wealth of the LDS church. Even on his deathbed, he only told one person where these mines were located—his wife. His son Caleb was then told by his mother where they were, but he never told a soul. Look to the western Uinta Mountains from Kamas to the Hanna area.

VERMONT

Bristol Spanish Gold

In 1752, the Spanish galleon San Jose was in the area. Four Spaniard deserters left the ship and took $80,000 in gold. Later the Spanish deserters were attacked by local Indians. Their pack horses were killed and they had to bury their gold between two large rocks in Hell's Half Acre near Bristol.

Lake Memphremagog Coins

During the Revolutionary War, a British cache of gold and silver was buried to keep it safe. Go detecting on the Southern shore of Lake Memphremagog. This is very near to Newport.

Indian Joe Worcester Mountain Gold

In the 1800s, an old Indian name Joe used to come in and buy supplies with gold dust and sometimes nuggets. After a time, outlaws caught on that he must have known a source of gold. They followed Joe to his hut in the woods of Worcester Mountain. They tried to spy on him, but he was too sneaky. Locals believe Joe found a rich lost gold mine in the area, which you could find today if you put in the work.

Smuggler's Notch Mystery Stashes

The area of Smuggler's Notch was used by almost every crook and outlaw in the old days. Some say there's a cave full of treasures. Others say the valley below has treasures of artifacts and little outlaw caches.

VIRGINIA

$63 Million Hidden In Bedford County

Thomas Beale made a lot of money mining gold and silver. Before Beale died, he created three ciphers pointing his family to his fortune. It's said he buried an amount equating to $65,000,000 in today's money. One cipher tells the location, the other tells about the contents of the treasure, and the last was the names of his next of kin. Utilize your local resources, find the ciphers, and go out on the hunt.

Mosby's Treasure In Virginia

Colonel John S. Mosby led a group of Confederates called the Mosby Raiders. They took a large treasure of gold, silver, and jewelry worth $350,000. Somewhere between the towns of Culpeper and Norman, close to route 522, it is said they buried the cache between two pine trees marked with an X. Later, his men were captured and killed, never having revealed the true location.

WASHINGTON

Buried Treasure Of Walla Walla County

A train robbery took place in the 1890s near Walla Walla, during which many gold bars were stolen. It was said the plan was to board a ship at Portland to escape, but that never happened. Instead, they had to bury the gold bars by Fort Walla Walla. Subsequent events saw the bandits shot dead before they could reveal the location of the gold.

Captain James Scarborough Treasure

James Allan became very wealthy and owned a lot of land on Chinook Point, along the Columbia River. It's said he buried $120,000 of gold in barrels close to his home. Both James and his wife died in 1852, without telling their family—or anyone else—where the treasure was buried on the property. Their son never found the gold.

Lars Hanson Treasure

A wealthy logger and businessman named Lars Hanson lived on Vashon Island in Puget Sound. He buried $200,000 in gold coins somewhere on the banks of Judd Creek, close to Burton. There are no records of gold treasures having been found in the area throughout the years, so there's a very good chance his hoard remains buried somewhere there still.

WEST VIRGINIA

Steamer Ship Treasure

Locals have reported finding silver coins washing up on the south bank of the river by Paden City. Many people think the coins are coming from a shipwreck or an old river boat steamer that you can see from the shore.

The Carpenter Farm Treasure

In the early 1930s, the United States of America sent out notices and documents forbidding people from hoarding gold of any type. People were forced to sell their gold at $20.67 per ounce to the Federal Reserve. During this time period, a farmer named Samuel Lawson is said to have buried $2,000 of gold and silver on the Carpenter Farm. This is located by Bear Fork, about nine miles east of Grantsville.

The Dennis Atkins Treasure

In 1900, a treasure of gold coins was buried by a man named Dennis Atkins. This treasure was worth $200,000, and is thought to be on the east banks of the Tug Fork River, just north of Kermit. Look for a toll bridge. Some locals say to start your search there.

WISCONSIN

John Dillinger's Buried Treasure

Dillinger was a bank robber who became a notoriously famous gangster. Before he died in 1934, he stole $300,000 worth of valuables. It is said Dillinger and Baby Face Nelson may have buried some of their loot. Use your local history archives to narrow down some clues to where and what.

The Lost Frederic Treasure

In 1895, Frederick Prentice buried a large cache. This cache is said to be near his home on Hermit Island in the Lake Superior area. His house is no longer standing, but I bet you could narrow down the location by researching in local library archives.

Balsam Lake Gold Wagon

There is a $200,000 gold treasure waiting to be found. Legend says gold miners were returning home from mining in Montana. In a swampy area, seven miles northeast of St. Croix and south of Balsam, the gold wagon sank in the mud due to heavy rains. Grab your metal detector and look for signs of an old trail to follow.

WYOMING

Lost Soldier Mine

The story goes that two soldiers somehow got separated from their troop. During this time, they wandered around trying to find their way back. One of the men found an ancient pickax and spade near a quartz ledge. On closer inspection, they could see the signs of mining work on the ledge. After returning to their unit, they told several others what they had found without telling them the exact location. They, of course, planned to return, but were unfortunately killed in the war.

The Sweetwater Lost Mine

Three prospectors were searching for minerals in the Sweetwater River's headwaters. They found enough gold ore to be encouraged. They returned home, then two of them returned to the prospecting area. Unfortunately, the two men were killed by local Indians. The location of their find remains a mystery.

Haystack Treasure Mine

I wish I had more on this tale, but I think a local could have some luck researching the legend. The story goes that a stranger saw an old prospector walking down from the mountain with his mule. The stranger walked up to the prospector and noticed he had a saddle bag of gold ore. When the stranger asked where he found the gold, the prospector pointed his finger in a direction and simply said, "Over there."

Last Remarks

I hope you're able to take some of the information presented in this book and find a treasure site in your area. Hopefully what you have read will provide you with ideas for clues, directions, locations, dollar amounts, and more. The legends in these pages are still out there waiting for someone like you to prove or disprove their veracity. I'm hoping you will let me know what you find as your own adventures progress. That way, I can keep a record of someone getting close and currently working on the site for posterity.

Image Index

Introductory Photo

1: The photo was taken by the author at Red Cliffs Reserve, St. George Utah (Old Spanish Carvings site)

Chapter 3: How To Look For Lost Records & Documents

1: Manuscript 512, Page One, published in 1753: Public domain image in country of origin(Brazil) and USA. (http://acervo.bndigital.bn.br/sophia/index.html) (https://commons.wikimedia.org/wiki/File:Manuscrito_512_01.jpg)
2: The photo was taken by the author at Parowan Gap, Utah (Native Indian Petroglyph Site)

Chapter 5: Treasure Clues Are Disappearing

1: Photo taken by the author, north of Beaver, Utah
2: Photo taken by the author, north of Servier, Utah
3: Photo taken by the author in the Pine Valley Public Land region of Utah (Lost silver mines and silver cache site location)
4: *Figure 1- Red rock monument overgrown.* Photo taken by the author west of Veyo, Utah (Old Spanish Massacre Site)
5: *Figure 2- Illustration of the rock monument. The pointer rock at the top shows the direction of travel.* Original illustration created for *Treasures of the Ancients*.

Chapter 6: Lost Cities In America

1: Arizona Gazette News Article April 5, 1909 "Explorations in Grand Canyon"
2: Tatahatso Point Map. Original illustration created for *Treasures of the Ancients*.
3: Codex Boturini, Folio 1: Public Domain image in both source country(Mexico) and US: From Boturini Codex Held at the National Museum of Anthropology in Mexico (Museo Nacional de Antropología (Mexico D.F.))(https://mna.inah.gob.mx/)(https://commons.wikimedia.org/wiki/File:Tira-1.JPG)
4: Codex Boturini, Folio 2: Public Domain in both source country(Mexico) and US: From Boturini Codex Held at the National Museum of Anthropology in Mexico (Museo Nacional de Antropología (Mexico D.F.))(https://mna.inah.gob.mx/) (https://commons.wikimedia.org/wiki/File:Boturini_Codex_(folio_2).JPG)

5: Map of Proposed Aztlan Territory before the 13th Century. Original illustration created for *Treasures of the Ancients*.

Chapter 7: Christopher Columbus And Early Explorers

1: Illustration of a Spanish Ship from the 1400s. Original illustration created for *Treasures of the Ancients*.
2: Unearthed Viking Ship: Public Domain in both source country(Germany) and US: From Nordische Fahrten. Skizzen und Studien, by Alexander Baumgartner. (https://www.flickr.com/photos/britishlibrary/11200273735) Held at The British Library (https://explore.bl.uk/primo_library/libweb/action/dlDisplay.do?vid=BLVU1&search_scope=LSCOP-ALL&docId=BLL01000231254&fn=permalink)

Chapter 8: Early Spanish Exploration

1: Old Spanish Waybill Document of the 1800s, referring to the Utah State, Uinta Mountains, recreated by the author
2: Old Spanish Map was drawn by Pedro Nunez in 1771, referring to the Uinta Mountains of Utah (Lost mines and buried caches -Treasures)
3: Photo of the author exploring a mine, north of Kamas, Utah (Known as the Yellow Jacket Mines)

Chapter 9: Transporting Treasure From Land To Sea

1-2: Photos taken by the author in the high Mountains of New Harmony, Utah (Old Mine discovered by author)

Chapter 10: Sunken Ships In The Caribbean

1: Photos taken by the author of an old bronze coin, dated in the 15th century - he discovered the coin in the Pine Valley Mountains region of Utah

Chapter 11: Using Lost History To Find Locations

1: Photo of the author, taken by Brandon Beneventi (used with permission) at the Old Iron Town Site of Southern Utah
2: Photo taken by the author of an old Spanish Smelter at Pine Valley Mountains, Utah Region
3: Photo taken by the author of Old Rock Monument Site in the Pinto, Utah region
4: Photo of the author at Mountain Meadows Massacre site of Utah (News interview picture with St. George News)
5: Photo taken by the author of the Mountain Meadows Memorial Site, Utah

6: Map of Mountain Meadows, Utah in the western United States: Public domain image sourced from Lights and shadows of Mormonism (Book) (https://archive.org/details/lightsandshadows00gib-buoft/page/n227/mode/2up)
(https://commons.wikimedia.org/wiki/File:Mountain-meadows-ut-us-map.png)
7: Photo taken by the author of the author's brother Brigham Draper in the Bull Valley Mountains of Utah

Chapter 12: Lost Mines And Prospecting

1: Illustration of a Spanish mine shaft as it would have looked. Original illustration created for *Treasures of the Ancients*.
2: Photo taken by the author at the old town site of Fisco, Utah - Old Ghost Town Ruins and mines
3: One of the twelve Mining Assays from the Area of Minerals and Old Spanish Mine issued by the author.
4: Photo of the author in the Hoyt Peak area of the Uinta Mountains, Utah
5: Photo taken by the author at Silver Reef, Utah (Old Mining & Ghost Town Site)

Chapter 13: Exploring Ghost Towns And Their Treasures

1: Photo taken by the author of an old ranch house along the Old Spanish Trail
2: Photo taken by the author at the site of movie set ruins of the "Gunsmoke TV Show" in Utah
3-4: Photos taken by the author outside of Mesquite, Nevada desert

Chapter 14: Get To Know Your Local History

1: Photo of the author, holding an old Spanish sword in Leeds, Utah

Chapter 15: Start Exploring And Learning The Terrain

1: Photo of the author, taken by Brigham Draper(used with permission), standing at an old Spanish Smelter in Southern Utah
2: Photo was taken in Washington, Utah at the author's home

Chapter 17: Rock Monuments And Written Inscriptions

1-4: Photos taken by Brandon Beneventi(used with permission), west of Salina, Utah
5-6 Photos taken by the author in the Lost Peak region of Utah

Chapter 18: Conclusions And Final Thoughts

1: Photos taken by the author in Cedar City, Utah

Chapter 19: Using Treasure Symbols As Clues

1: Graphic of treasure hunting symbols. Original illustration created for *Treasures of the Ancients*.
2: Photo taken by Brandon Beneventi(used with permission) at an old Spanish mine site in the Uinta Mountains, Utah
3: Photo taken by the author in the Samak, Utah region
4: Photo of the author at Old Spanish King Mine site in Uinta Mountains of Utah
5: Photo taken by the author in the Uinta Mountain Range of Utah
6: Photo of the author by an old tree carving in the Uinta Mountains of Yellow Pine, Utah
7: Recreated photo taken by the author with notes taken west of Veyo, Utah
8: Photo taken by the author in the desert of Kanab, Utah
9: Photo taken by the author at Fort Pierce, Utah ruins site
10: Photo taken by the author at Loins Mouth historical site of Utah
11: Photo taken by Jada Johnson (Jada Lee Photos) Hawaii(used with permission)
12-13: Photo taken by the author at Chichen Itza, Mexico
14-15: Photo taken by the author at Gunlock, Utah - Paiute Native Indian Region
16: Photo of the author, south desert of Green River, Utah
17: Photo taken by LeeAnn Draper(used with permission) at Werner Valley, Utah
18: Photo taken by the author of an old smelter from a mine created in the early 1900s
19: Photo of the author at an old Spanish carvings site
20: Photo taken by the author on the eastern mountain slopes of Kamas, Utah

About the Author

1: Photo of the author at "Lion's Mouth," Native Indian Historical Site of Utah

Be on the lookout for the second book:

BEYOND THE CATTLE GATE: OUTLAW HISTORY, LEGENDS, AND TREASURE

COMING IN LATE 2023

About the Author

Timothy Draper at a Sacred Ancient Native American Site

Timothy Draper was born in Mesa, Arizona, in 1978. At the age of 12, he developed a passion for adventure in the outdoors and history. By the time he was 18, he had already embarked on many adventures exploring ghost towns and searching for lost Spanish mines.

Timothy spent most of his adult life working in construction and venturing out in the wilderness in his free time. Later, he attended college and universities where he studied anthropology and history. He started working with film producers and major networks in 2015, and has been involved in numerous TV shows focused on treasure hunting.

In 2018, Timothy became the founder of Treasures in America, selling treasure hunting gear, and consulting with many people regarding their personal treasure hunts. In 2021, he also became the founder of the *Uncharted Expedition* web series that features real-life treasure hunting sites and situations. The show is available on many platforms.

Timothy enjoys a good hunt and spends every chance he gets in the desert or high mountains chasing after his next big discovery. He tells everyone he'll continue to search until the day he is no longer physically able to.

www.ingramcontent.com/pod-product-compliance
Lightning Source LLC
Chambersburg PA
CBHW050518170426
43201CB00013B/2003